WHAT HAPPENED TO SWEDEN?

– while America became
the only superpower.

Ulf Nilson

WHAT HAPPENED TO SWEDEN?

– while America became the only superpower.

NORDSTJERNAN

Förlag, New York

Nordstjernan Förlag, New York 2007

www.nordstjernan.com

WHAT HAPPENED TO SWEDEN?
– while America became the only superpower.
Copyright © 2007 Ulf Nilson
Copy edit: Bo Zaunders, Amanda Robison.
Cover photograph: Duncan Walker
Cover design: Ulf Mårtensson
Typeface: Body, Berling; Headlines, Anziano by Fountain
ISBN: 0-9672176-4-4
First Edition, September 2007
Printed in the United States of America

Nordstjernan Förlag
Book Services
P.O. Box 1710
New Canaan, CT 06840

CONTENTS

Author's Note

This book is in no way an academic work. It is rather a journey through the history of my two countries: Sweden, where I was born, and the US, where I lived for twenty years. The purpose is to show how ordinary citizens are formed by their country's history, and the system, meaning the way or ways of life, its liberties, and restrictions. As the reader will notice right at the start, the ambition has not been to write an exhaustive history but rather to sketch the development, first in very broad strokes, and later, as we come to more contemporary times, in more detail. Since the US is, for obvious reasons - size, power, etc. - so much better known than Sweden, I have gone into much more detail as far as the latter country is concerned. I have, to put it in another way, tried to make the picture of Sweden clearer by contrasting it to the, admittedly, much less detailed picture of America.

The book is also, in a small way, an autobiography.

As a correspondent for the Swedish evening paper *Expressen*, I covered the US, including Vietnam during the war years. I marched in the civil rights marches in the 60's, interviewed Martin Luther King as well as Deputy Sheriff Cecil Price in Philadelphia, Mississippi (who helped perpetrate the murder of three young civil rights workers). I met presidents Kennedy, Johnson, Nixon and Reagan—meaning that I shook hands with them. A Swedish correspondent is by definition a small-timer in Washington and the access to men and women of real power was very limited in spite of the well-known and wonderful American openness.

I covered, sometimes crying over my typewriter, the assassinations of JFK, King, and Robert Kennedy; I went to Vietnam fifteen times and was close to death there and in other places of conflict more than once.

During my time as correspondent, I traveled some 200 days a year (more than the number of working days for an ordinary Swede), and fell in love with New Orleans, San Francisco, and of course, the capital of the world, which is undoubtedly New York. I saw Neil Armstrong and Buzz Aldrin dance on the moon that fantastic summer night in 1969, followed a long row of presidential campaigns and an even longer row of summit meetings, including that surrealistic encounter between Reagan and Gorbachev in Iceland. I became an unabashed fan of the American political system: the vitality, the hoopla, and, not the least, the virtuosity of political reporters and commentators, be they in print, radio or TV. I was happy enough to get to report on all of Muhammad Ali's championship fights (yes, my friend you are the Greatest!) as well as quite a few of Mike Tyson's. As this book hopefully shows, I also read much, watched lots of TV, and talked every day to those we call (certainly for lack of a better word) ordinary Americans. I wrote several books about the US and my experiences there.

I lived in Sweden until the age of 30, when I went to New York as a correspondent. It didn't take me long to decide that, if at all possible, I would not return to live permanently in my home country, where I have family and friends and where my three daughters were born.

When I left for the New World (where I had never set foot before) I was already a pretty well-known journalist in Sweden, indeed that was the reason I was picked for a post that was considered most important. Already at the age of 23 I had covered the Hungarian uprising (seeing for the first time dead and mutilated bodies). In the coming decades, I worked first in New York, then out of Paris, then again New York and later once again Paris, all the time traveling the world. I discovered, or more importantly, I helped my readers discover the new China, Brazil, Egypt, Israel, war-torn Lebanon, women's conditions around the globe, the new face of Communism, and much more.

Of great import, as far as this book is concerned, is that I spent every summer in Sweden with my family, covering various events and interviewing important people. I dealt with politicians as well as industrialists, businessmen, artists, authors, and, of course, media men and women, even a few criminals. The country is small, its establishment even smaller. It is fair to say that everybody knows everybody, and that all major decisions are taken within a group of perhaps 50-100 people, almost all of them men. I can safely say that I have come to know over the years almost all of the movers and shakers, some of them (like Olof Palme, who figures a lot in this book) quite well, others mainly by reputation and mutual acquaintance. If this sounds like bragging, I can only repeat that Sweden is a very small country, heavily centered on Stockholm, with quite a few journalists who could make the same claims as I have made. Some colleagues, based in Stockholm, got so close to the people they were supposed to cover, that it became rather ridiculous to speak of objectivity or even fairness. As I note in the book, two thirds or more of the media people in the country consider themselves leftist in one form or another. Guess which party line has an easier time in front of klieg lights and reporters…

The reason I write all this is to make clear my vantage point. When it comes to Sweden, I have seen it both from the inside and from far away. I went to school in Slöinge on the west coast, a very small village, and in the nearby city of Falkenberg, where I got my first job as a journalist at the age of 17, mainly writing obituaries and birthday notices. At least it taught me to use the typewriter. I experienced the wonderful 1950's, when you could be hired and fired and then rehired by somebody else in the very same day. I experienced the increasingly intrusive social engineering first hand at grass root level and, only a few years later, got to see what was known as Sweden, the middle way, the Swedish Experiment or the Swedish Model. I did this with eyes that had also seen other continents and countries where human beings tried to live together or annihilate each other in so much more dramatic ways.

In 1995, I was summarily fired as a columnist for the newspaper *Expressen* (where I had spent 32 years) because of my political views, which are mildly center-right and very strongly against Communism and other extreme ideologies. A couple of years later I was rehired and am, as of this writing, in my fourth year as a born again commentator. I also write a weekly column for the oldest Swedish American newspaper, *Nordstjernan* in New York, a job I cherish.

At last, the reader should note that while I quite frequently quote people and publications, I have not bothered with footnotes or indexes. This is to make the book an easier read, and to let the reader feel that he or she is free to check and question absolutely everything.

I know full well that in Sweden this book, if it is read at all, will be considered revisionist and quite possibly extremist. So be it. Just the same, I think I should end this introduction by saying the following:

I am not out to convince anybody about anything. In history and politics the last word is never said, nor written.

Ulf Nilson

March, 2007

1

The beginning

When Columbus sailed the ocean blue in 1492, Sweden was already on its way to becoming one of the first centralized nation states in the world (which was at the time more or less the same as Europe, at least to the Europeans). It was also on its way to becoming a great power.

By coincidence in 1492, an earlier great power was crumbling. The Muslim Moors, primarily Arabs, were driven out of what is now Spain. It took until the early 2000's before fundamentalist Islamic groups, such as the terrorist organization al-Qaida, reclaimed all the areas ever under Muslim rule. By that time the followers of Allah had returned in force to countries all over Europe, mainly as refugees or what is called economic immigrants; in other words, they were people looking for ways to support themselves. This created problems (described later on), not the least in Sweden, which was, up to the later part of the 20th century, one of the most homogenous nations in the world.

The United States of course, did not exist, and probably no more than a very tiny handful of Swedes got to know, before much later, that a new world had been discovered: a world that would save the old world from its follies and eventually dominate it.

The fact that Nordic seafarers—most likely from what became Norway and Iceland—had landed in America a couple of hundred years earlier, was also forgotten, and maybe better so.

According to historian Daniel Boorstein, the Vikings quite soon concluded that life was too difficult on the new continent. The country was rich, but the redskins were both hostile and well armed, so the bold Scandinavians decided to fold tents and go home, not to come back in numbers until the 19th and 20th centuries, and then it was to work, not to conquer.

What if they had stayed? Would the language they spoke, whatever it was, have been as much in use as English is today?

Most likely not, but who can say for sure?

Instead of going west, the Swedes looked eastward. That's the reason the small, Nordic country became a great power, indeed almost a superpower, long before the US existed. This might sound irrelevant in a book dealing with conditions as they are today, but I think it is the other way around. To some extent, the fact that Sweden's days of conquest and glory are over colors the relationship even in our days. The same goes for other countries in Europe, like Great Britain, France, and Germany, all more dominant than Sweden. To have been bypassed by history and made dependent on a country far away simply doesn't feel good.

And today everybody is to some extent dependent on the US.

A very brief history of Sweden, really only a few points of reference, will show what I mean. This is what we were, long before the West was won or even discovered.

The Vikings, most likely Swedish ones, traveling east (*i Österled*) are said to have founded what became Russia - which went on to be for 74 years the Soviet Union, and is today once again Russia. Long before Sweden existed as a country, the Swedes established themselves as warriors, bent principally on war and looting as well as trade. They lived short, brutish lives, often born in places they left as teenagers, and were never to see again. After Sweden proper was united, or almost, by King Gustaf Vasa in the early 16th century, it didn't take long for the Swedes to build up a great empire, deep down into what would become Germany, Poland, and upwards into what is now the Baltic countries (Estonia, Latvia, and Lithuania) as well as Finland. During the hundred years between 1560 and 1660, the empire never ceased to expand. It was by default of communication and administrative difficulties a very loosely held together organism, much unlike the American colonies (see page 25). Orders from the king in Stockholm took months to reach cities like Riga or Reval (today Tallinn) and quite often didn't arrive at all. Governors and military commanders could rule pretty much as they liked, provided they collected taxes and now and then conscripted soldiers. Common folks, one could say, lived more or less under occupation.

On the other hand, one could very well say the same for most people in the mother country.

The reasons the Vikings and later Swedish conquerors looked mainly to the East were primarily two:

One, resistance was not that strong. Peter the Great did not enter the scene until the early 18th century, and the small countries on the fringes of Russia were too weak to be much of a match for the conquering Swedes whose armies were, for centuries, composed of as many foreigners as Swedes. Indeed, for a long time, officers, even if they were Swedes, gave their commands in some kind of German.

Two, and perhaps more important, the southern part of Sweden (mainly the provinces of Skåne, Halland, and Blekinge), was still Danish. To reach it from Stockholm a traveler or an army had to cross through the wilderness of the Kolmården and other great and dangerous forests, filled with robbers, beasts, diseases, darkness, and probably also ghosts, witches, and devils. Where the forests began the world more or less ended. So much better then, to travel by ship over the usually calm and inviting Baltic.

The Danes, for the same reasons crossed the Öresund to occupy the Swedish provinces mentioned above as well as great swaths of what became Norway. During the reign of King Christian II, whom the Danes called The Good and the Swedes called The Tyrant, the Danes actually conquered Stockholm but were relatively promptly driven back, never to return. Before leaving, Christian II had a good part of the Swedish nobility decapitated—the reason for the tyrant epithet. The lack of a strong class of noble men in turn made it easier for Gustaf Vasa to gather so much power in his own hands. It also made Swedish peasants much more independent than their counterparts on the European continent.

Sweden became a Protestant country (following the teachings of Martin Luther) under Gustaf Vasa, who, among other things wanted to get his hands on church land and treasure (as much as possible to add to his own immense collection; Gustaf was, without doubt, the greediest king Sweden ever had and was also probably the richest Swede of all times, relatively speaking). According to Encyclopedia Britannica the king was not a very pleasant man, but suspicious, mendacious, cruel, vengeful, demagogic, and capricious, a description you would certainly not find reading Swedish schoolbooks, but evidently quite close to the truth. In school we learned rather that Gustaf was good looking, kind, generous, and a friend of farmers and other common folks. This is highly unlikely. Many of his advisers were indeed imported from Germany.

Religion was one of the two main reasons Sweden became involved in the great Thirty Years' War, which devastated Central Europe (mainly what is now Germany) for three decades, killing, on a proportional basis considerably more people than the two great conflagrations of the 20th century and actually matching the plague of the 14th century, which in its turn did as much damage as an all out atomic war would do.

Or so some experts, including famed historian Barbara Tuchman, speculate.

The second reason was, of course, politics.

Together with France and to some extent England, Sweden was continental Europe's leading power. As Henry Kissinger notes in his "Diplomacy," the Swedish Army of the time, counting 90,000 men, was the largest in the world. It was commanded from the outset by one of Sweden's two hero kings, Gustaf II Adolf. The Lion from the North as he was widely known, certainly wanted to defend the (in his eyes) only true Christian belief against the Pope and his cohorts. But it's almost certain that in his heart of hearts he was equally determined to expand his empire and continue to play a major role on, what was then, the world stage—in other words, to be the big guy on the block.

The fact that commanders of great armies became very rich (at least as long as they were victorious) certainly played a role. Sweden was a poor peasant nation and certainly not cultured; to find paintings, statues, books, and other treasures, you had to look south.

Gustaf Adolf was very fat and moved with some difficulty. He led his troops personally, mounted on a specially selected horse. He was brave and ruthless, which a king simply had to be in these days, and he didn't shrink from taking part in hand-to-hand combat. This led to his death on the 6th of November 1632, on a battlefield close to the German city of Lützen, where he was brutally slaughtered, much to the joy of the enemies. In Sweden he became the greatest of heroes to generation after generation of admiring school children (boys born on the 6th of November are still sometimes baptized Gustaf Adolf).

During the rest of the war, which lasted until 1648, when the Westphalian Peace was concluded, the Swedish Army was under the command of Johan Banér and later Lennart Torstensson, both counts, both extremely interested in killing and even more in looting. Banér was particularly cruel, indeed a swine in our terms, but then, generals at the time of the 30 Years' War were not supposed to be nice, neither to friend nor foe. The same went for ordinary soldiers: the killing of defenseless opponents was routine and civilians were slaughtered, both to get hold of their possessions and for the sheer fun of it. Rape, of course, was common.

This, of course, is very conveniently forgotten, when Swedes complain about the treatment of slaves in the US as well as the extermination of the Native Americans. (Which was, as French essayist Jean-Francois Revel has pointed out, committed by newly arrived Europeans.)

Both Torstensson and Banér and many of their underlings amassed great fortunes of stolen gold, silver, paintings, and the like. Indeed, when the treasures of the Swedish Court (*Livrustkammaren*) were exhibited in Washington in 1988, a review in the *Washington Post* stated that the most remarkable fact was that not even one of the objects exhibited was made in Sweden: each was stolen, principally during the Thirty Years' War.

The reviewer, who was of Austrian origin, concluded:

"Maybe that is one of the reasons Austrian grand mothers even today admonish their grandchildren with the words: 'Be nice, mein kind, otherwise the Swede will come and get you.'"

The second of the great hero kings, Charles XII came to power, meaning absolute power, in 1697. He was fifteen years old and well educated but of course without experience. He either detested women or was frightened stiff when they approached him; he never married and was probably a homosexual even if this was never noted (at least not on paper) by his contemporaries.

Sweden was thrown into war two years after Charles' ascension to the throne, presumably to the King's satisfaction, since military matters were his only true interests (if you exclude riding, hunting, and playing violent and often tasteless pranks). He was trained and ready and absolutely convinced of his own God-given right to command and decide. In 1700, he left Stockholm to wage war on the Continent and against Russia. According to his most famous biographer, Voltaire, the first time he heard the sound of bullets zinging by, he asked a fellow officer:

"What's that sound?"

"Bullets."

Whereupon the King exclaimed:

"This will henceforth be my music!"

All this according to Voltaire, who might have made it up.

Charles never returned to Stockholm, where a palace was being built for him, a formidable building that he took great interest in but never got to see. Until his death 18 yeas later, he spent most of his time on foreign soil, always in uniform, always planning or executing military operations. Ordinary working Swedes probably didn't interest him; anyway, after the age of 17 he hardly saw an ordinary, civilian Swede.

In 1700, Charles won a great victory against the Russians in the Battle of Narva and set out to conquer Moscow. Instead the Russian tactics of scorched earth in connection with an unusually cold winter conquered the Swedes like it later defeated Napoleon and Hitler. When I went to school in the late 1940's, we had to learn how to draw the map of the battleground and the distribution of forces, as well as explain why the Swedes were so superior. The teacher always stressed that it was the courage of the King, as well as his superior strategic sense, that gave us victory.

However, the winning streak didn't last long. In 1709, Charles' great rival for power in the north, Czar Peter, won a decisive battle at Poltava, a very important turning point for both powers; after Poltava, Sweden would successively shrink in size and importance, while Russia began its slow march upward, forming an empire and finally gaining super power status before collapsing and starting anew.

The majority of the Swedes who fought at Poltava became prisoners of war; Charles had to flee to Bender, Turkey where he spent nearly five years trying to govern very far away Sweden, whilst at the same time persuading the Turks to go to war against Peter (who got to be called The Great after 1721). The Turks made some half-hearted attempts to take up arms but were discouraged or possibly bought off. Nothing important happened.

When Charles fled from the defeat at Poltava, Sweden ceased being a great power, even if this was not immediately recognized. Like a burnt out star, the light of which is still visible, it fascinated many in Europe, not the least because of the personality of the King. To many he was a romantic figure, mysterious and fascinating. In reality, however, the rest of Charles' life was but a long, terribly bloody, and wasteful epilog. He managed to get back to Sweden in 1714, riding horseback across the Continent. In spite of the fact that the Swedish hold over parts of Germany had collapsed, leading to loss of revenue, Charles chose to go to war against far away Norway. That war went very badly, and in 1718 a bullet, possibly fired by one of his own soldiers or officers, killed Charles. According to myth the bullet was made from a silver button from the king's coat; a bullet that meets the description has for many years been on display at a museum in the city of Varberg, Sweden.

The bullet story has definitely not been confirmed. Regardless of that, and much more important, is the fact that the long string of wars fought not only by Gustav II Adolf and Charles XII but also by the Swedish Kings Charles X and Charles XI, bled the country dry. Indeed, when the Kings and their armies fought and marauded on the Continent and in Russia, common folks in the home country were starving and suffering, plagued by ever-stiffer demands by the far off headquarters. The time of Charles XII was particularly disastrous and it would hardly be wrong to claim that rather than being a hero, he was a war crazed madman, albeit aided and abetted in his insanity by both supporters and adversaries that were pretty much of the same ilk. It might well have been correct to let Charles go down in history as the worst king the country ever had.

However, that's not how history works.

Nations have memories, formed by tradition and education and enhanced by what can only be called indoctrination.

Gustaf II Adolf, who did so much to destroy Central Europe, who commanded troops that raped, murdered, and stole, who was indifferent to the suffering of common people, who, indeed, helped terrorize a great part of the European continent, this horrible man, in Swedish history books became The Lion from the North, a staunch defender of the one and only true faith. Most historians, certainly those who wrote the school text books, failed to mention that The Lion was heavily subsidized by none other than Jean Armand du Plessis, also known as Cardinal Richelieu, maybe France's greatest statesman up to the time of de Gaulle and, of course, a defender of Catholicism, precisely the faith that Gustaf II Adolf was fighting against.

The reasons the two were cooperating were rather simple. Richelieu, who might or might not have been a religious man, wanted the various German princes to fight each other as long as possible—in other words, stay divided and weak. The Swedish King, well paid for his efforts, did France's dirty work for it.

"He (Richelieu) probably delayed the creation of a German state by 200 years," Kissinger writes, admiringly.

Since then, France (and the rest of the world), as we know all too well, has had a few problems with united Germany. Europe left on its own, "losing" wars in 1870, 1914, and 1939, respectively. The two latter ones led to Europe's demise as the power center of the world and the coming of the US and the Soviet Union.

Swedish schools teach very little of this; in my days, history lessons were nothing but pure and undiluted chauvinism. The Hero King was wise, brave, deeply Christian (in the right manner), and really without fault. He made Sweden the strongest power on Earth (well, almost). Our word counted all around the known world. A Swede was definitely more than a Pole or Russian, not to mention people who came from what was later to become Italy or Germany. We were admired and feared. Admittedly we paid heavily in blood and treasure but we won more battles than we lost and dominated the Baltic Sea totally.

In brief, to be a Swede really MEANT something!

I should add, that among old folks (and Sweden is demographically one of the world's oldest countries), what I just wrote still stands. We were once the greatest. Now somebody else is, namely the US, and maybe not surprisingly many dislike this fact very much.

Charles XII won his last major battle on the 4th of July 1708, in Holowczyn, Poland. He went on fighting unsuccessfully for another ten years and would most likely have continued for yet another ten or more, had that bullet in Norway not stopped him.

In the process, the country was ruined, the population decimated, and the possibilities of holding on to the empire nullified. Sweden, a classical example of what historian Paul Kennedy calls imperial overstretch, had bitten off far more than it could chew. Some saw it, but many more did not, perhaps in part because Charles's youth, his simple habits, and mysterious sexuality (or perhaps lack of it) fascinated his contemporaries. A steady stream of propaganda helped them, from Stockholm as well as the King's headquarters, and by quite a few independent authors.

Daniel Defoe (of *Robinson Crusoe* fame) wrote a glowing book about Charles, stressing the opinion that the King was both humane and just, which was most certainly not true. Dr. Samuel Johnson, who should, perhaps, have known better, made him a paragon of honesty and decisiveness. But the work that really would influence the world's image of Charles XII, was written by no less a man than Voltaire, Europe's leading intellectual of the time (in spite of his truly terrible flattery of Catharine the Great in Russia and other rich benefactors). His work, *Histoire de Charles XII, roi de Suède*, has been printed in countless editions and read by millions of people, particularly in Europe. It has been claimed that only two other books have reached so many readers: the Bible and John Bunyan's The Pilgrim's Progress. The main reason was undoubtedly that Charles fascinated his times, achieving a mythical status, and admired even by people who had not the slightest idea of where Sweden was located. In words that have become classic, Voltaire portrays the King as a man larger than life:

"He is perhaps the only human being and up to now the only king, who has lived without weakness… His great qualities, of which a single one could have made another prince immortal, became a disaster for his country… He wanted to win empires to give them away…a unique human being rather than a great man, worthy of admiration, rather than imitation…"

Apparently Voltaire was by no means an uncritical admirer, but over the years the criticism wore off while the admiration stayed. We wanted it that way. And not many Swedes ever read what Winston Churchill wrote about The Hero King in his work about the Duke of Marlborough. Churchill described Charles as a gambler, rather than a strategist, an adventurer, rather than a statesman.

He was, in other words, irresponsible.

For most Swedes, however, one fact remains. Under Charles XII, Sweden was bigger and, at least to begin with, more powerful than ever before. Sweden was 'it' and had been so for a long time. This feeling continued to play a role, albeit steadily diminishing, until the union with Norway (which had been forced on the Norwegians), was dissolved in 1805. At that time the famous Swedish neutrality had been born, largely through the foresight and strategic realism of one Jean Baptiste Bernadotte, one of Napoleon's marshals (albeit perhaps the lousiest one as far as military matters were concerned). Bernadotte was elected crown prince of Sweden during the unsettled period after Charles XII, and went on to become King Carl XIV Johan.

Carl Johan was first and foremost a very cautious man. He was more or less forced to go to war against Napoleon's France and later attacked first Denmark, then Norway with the intention to make himself king over the latter country. The plan succeeded, and this after a brief and almost bloodless campaign in 1814.

At the congress of Vienna in 1815 Carl XIV Johan, not a humble man, put himself forward as a possible ruler of post Napoleon France. The victorious powers, however, were not going to allow another general to become the leader of the defeated country, and his efforts were blocked.

More important, in this context, is the fact that the war against Norway was Sweden's last. The country is now fast approaching 200 years of peace, neutrality, and introspection.

To this, I shall return. Suffice it here to say that the United States were still not very united. Indeed the better part of what is now the world's only superpower was barely populated. The leading colonial power was the United Kingdom, but France had its share, as did indeed Sweden...

At the time of the Declaration of Independence and the founding of the USA in 1776, Sweden's population was a little over 2 million inhabitants. The USA at the same time had a population of close to 4 million, of which almost 700,000 were slaves. The Native Americans were never counted.

Of the European settlers in the New World, 60 percent came from England, 80 percent from Great Britain and the remainder came from Germany and Holland. Close to all, 98 percent, were Protestant.

The two countries were comparable in size and, not considering Native Americans or slaves, extremely homogenous.

2

America expanding

The expression 'Manifest Destiny' first appeared in a magazine article by John L. O'Sullivan, who wrote that it is the "fulfillment of our manifest destiny to overspread the continent allotted by Providence..."

The operative words are allotted by providence, meaning that God himself meant that Americans, that is, the white ones that came from Europe, were preordained to inhabit the new continent; that they were, indeed, the chosen people, or at least a chosen people. It also meant that whoever stood in the way for the expansion was, by definition, an enemy.

O'Sullivan's piece was published in July 1845. 'Manifest Destiny' immediately became a catch phrase, the thing for politicians, journalists, and adventurous folks of all stripes to say. In short, the people who wanted to conquer and expand. In fact, however, the territorial expansion of the United States had started much, much earlier, actually long before there even was a United States.

And even before Sweden started to shrink.

At the beginning, there was stiff competition, very stiff, for the ownership of the new world, as well as for Asia and Africa, indeed for all the territories discovered by seafarers like Diaz, Vasco da Gama, Christopher Columbus, and others. The world had grown. The supply of riches seamed unlimited and everybody with imagination and resources wanted to partake in the loot.

The Spaniards, who think they discovered America (although Columbus was from Genoa, Italy), took possession of most of what is now Latin America. They also colonized Florida in 1513 and New Mexico in 1540, but in due course lost to various Latin American nations and the US.

The Spaniards killed and maimed people who stood in their way. They brought home with them vast fortunes of silver, gold, and diamonds. The most important thing they found, however, was almost certainly the potato. In 1531 when the Spanish conquistador Pizarro brought down the Incan Empire in what is now Peru, he and his men found potatoes and learned to eat them.

The potato crossed the Atlantic and changed world history. Frederick the Great's Prussia might have lost the Seven Years' War if the country's peasants had not had potatoes to eat. The Irish might not have emigrated to the US in such incredible numbers if the potato pest had not struck Ireland. And so on. Indeed, it could probably be argued that the humble potato is the most important product ever imported to Europe from the new world.

The first permanent British colony, Jamestown, named for a king, was founded in 1607. Then came the New England colonies; subsequently New York, New Jersey, and Delaware were taken from the Dutch by force of arms in 1664.

Like its archrival Great Britain, France had the ambition to rule as much of the world as possible. The French established themselves in scattered settlements in the Mississippi Valley, controlling the great river and the soon extremely important port city of New Orleans. The French first arrived in 1673 (quite some time after the Swedes) but were not finally kicked out until 90 years later. France, of course, also conquered the part of Canada that is now Quebec, which is still French speaking, kind of.

So, the race was on. But there was still no talk of 'Manifest Destiny,' and nobody, at least as far as I know, had any idea that the descendants of the ragged settlers would be, a little more than 300 years or some ten generations later, the citizens of the world's only superpower.

It took many years of dangerous and often ruthless expansion, a string of wars, and one breathtakingly brazen diplomatic bluff to make the US fit to play among the big guys, still the United Kingdom, France and, after 1870, more and more Germany, which in the next century would play the leading role in Europe's two attempts to commit suicide.

The world was still very, very Euro-centric; London and Paris were the cities that really counted, all the rest were provincial, even if Rome, Florence, Venice, and Berlin continued to attract business people, students, and other visitors. As for Washington, today's imperial capital, it did not exist until the end of the 18th century and didn't become the capital until 1800, when Congress met there for the first time. (It continued to be quite provincial well into the middle of the 20th century; a city of Southern efficiency and Northern charm, said John F. Kennedy as late as 1961.)

In 1775, the rebellion against British rule had broken out, the first of the three great revolutions in modern times (followed by the French in 1789, and the Russian in 1917). In 1776, the Declaration of Independence was written and from1780-82 the Continental Congress laid the foundation for the United States.

In 1781, The Congress elected John Hanson of Maryland as the President of the United States in Congress assembled. As Hanson happened to be of Swedish ancestry it is often said that the first president of the US was actually Swedish. This is not quite correct. The presiding officer during the deliberations, Hanson, whose statue stands on Capitol Hill, was no doubt influential and well respected, but without power. President in the true sense of the word, he was not.

After the War of Liberation was won, the expansion continued at an almost feverish pace. In 1803, when Napoleon dominated Europe (and thus the world), the third US president, Thomas Jefferson, decided that the new nation needed the Louisiana Territories to facilitate the conquest of the West. The French had earlier ceded the Territories to Spain, but Napoleon took it back. Jefferson now sent an emissary to Napoleon's foreign minister, the legendary Talleyrand, but the negotiations came to naught. Jefferson decided on a second attempt at which a new emissary hinted darkly that maybe, just maybe, the US might ally itself with Britain, against France. Napoleon, who was not very interested in the New World, didn't realize that he was being had. The last thing he wanted was the US to team up with Britain and a deal was struck.

That deal, in fact, was a steal, probably the most successful real estate transaction in human history, looked upon from the buyer's point of view. For exactly $27,267,622, the world's then newest country got no less than 828,000 square miles (2,144,520 km2) of land, cities, villages, people, cattle, and of course, control of the mighty Mississippi.

Here, we might do well to pause for a moment and ask the eternal question: What if it had not happened?

What if Napoleon, brilliant as he certainly was, had realized the potential of the new world? What if he had held on to Louisiana and the rest of the Purchase territory? What if, in one way or the other, there would have been one English America, basically Protestant, and one Catholic France (becoming more and more secular)? Would there in time have been war? Would the influence of Latin America have become more pervasive north of the border?

Impossible to say, of course.

Napoleon was first and foremost a European, even if he realized the strategic importance of North Africa. The world was Europe. He wanted to rule it and pretty much did. As far as the so-called New World was concerned, he opted for the money (which he badly needed for his wars) rather than the chance to expand.

The Purchase made the US grow in area by almost five Swedens, which was at the time, and still is one of the largest countries in Europe, second only to France or Spain. (A large part of Sweden, particularly along the border with Norway is hardly habitable.)

Around the time of the Louisiana Purchase, Sweden was in turmoil. In 1792, King Gustaf III was murdered after a fairly unsuccessful war against Russia and an all too successful attempt to gain absolute power. The King was vain and haughty and much hated by nobility whose most important members decided that he had to be eliminated. The assassination took place during a masked ball in Stockholm, later the inspiration for Verdi's opera "The Masked Ball" (which is by far better known today than the event that inspired it).

At the time of the assassination, the heir to the throne was still a minor and the country was ruled for some years by one G. A. Reuterholm, a ruthless and power hungry fellow, who is sometimes called Sweden's only dictator (although quite a few kings were, in fact, dictators, too). Once Reuterholm was booted out and driven into exile, Gustaf IV Adolf took the throne. He didn't do too well. Sweden went to war against Napoleon in 1805 as a part of the third European coalition. This was a bit unlucky because when France and Russia made peace at Tilsit in 1807, Russia was free to settle scores with Sweden, its archenemy since some hundred years back.

A brief war followed. Sweden was outgunned and had to sue for peace. It cost Sweden the possession of Finland and Gustaf IV Adolf the throne he really never should have had.

The brother of Gustaf III, who took the name Karl XIII, succeeded him. He was a weak and listless ruler, quite unable to realize how small the country had become. The Swedes were poor as ever, and at least in so-called leading circles, in a state of shock. Nations have long memories, and after all, only around a hundred years earlier, Sweden had been no marginal player but one of the truly great powers. Ordinary folks most likely didn't much care, but in ruling circles one thought differently...

A Danish prince was elected Crown Prince, but he died soon after the election and was replaced with Jean Baptist Bernadotte, Marshal of France, elected in 1810 and king from 1817. His wife, Desiree, also known as Napoleon's great love, became queen of Sweden, but detested the country and spent very little time there. The climate was simply too harsh and as for culture, well even when ruled by a French marshal, Stockholm was no Paris.

When Bernadotte became king, under the name Carl XIV Johan, Sweden had a new constitution (adopted in 1809) which gave him full executive power but stated that his decisions had to be countersigned (i.e. agreed too) by a state council. Much as the US House of Representatives, the Parliament (Riksdagen) got exclusive right of taxation, a right it has enthusiastically exercised, with the result that the Swedes today have the somewhat dubious distinction of being the heaviest taxed individuals on Earth.

To sum it all up:

At the time of the Louisiana Purchase, when the US expansion started in earnest, Sweden was in full decline as a great and influential power.

It would continue on that track.

The next great American land grab came in 1845 and led to a war with Mexico. The Americans took control over Texas. President James Polk sent John Slidell as an emissary to Mexico City—undoubtedly with the successful Louisiana Purchase in fresh memory—to negotiate and buy New Mexico and California, both Mexican territories, for up to 30 million dollars. But Slidell was snubbed. Instead, the Mexicans attacked and war was inevitable, something that did not make the American side all too unhappy.

The war lasted two years, from 1846-48. It went America's way and when it ended, New Mexico, Utah, Nevada, Arizona, California and Texas were added to the US. Cost: 15 million dollars. Mexico lost around half of its territory, and then thousands of Americans set out to settle the West, evicting the Indians on their way and forcing them to live on ever less attractive reservations. Even before that, in 1823, President James Monroe had stated his principles, much later known as the Monroe Doctrine, which say that there should be no further colonization of the New World and that the US should abstain from involvement in European affairs, while the governments of Europe should practice non-intervention in the affairs of the Western Hemisphere. The Monroe Doctrine is still observed even if the US (luckily) saw fit to intervene in the two World Wars, as well as the long Cold War that succeeded them.

While this went on, industry began to grow in the northern states, while the South remained agricultural, which meant plantations dependent on slaves. States´ rights to manage their own affairs became a serious issue. Friction and soon hostility followed - particularly after President Abraham Lincoln denied the southern states the right to secede from the Union. Eventually, the Civil War came. It need not be reported here. Suffice it to say that:

1.   The North won and with it the Union and the Federal government in Washington, DC.

2.   It meant in itself a kind of a land grab in as much that the outcome consolidated the US as ONE country, which would never more risk being divided or splintered.

However, one of the main objectives of the North was *not* achieved. The slaves were set free, true, but really only on paper. In the South and to a very large extent in the North, too, segregation remained the order of the day, legally for another hundred years or so, and in practice much longer.

The buying of territory continued in 1867, when Alaska was bought from Russia. Several years before that, in 1851, Hawaii had placed itself under US protection (it became fully American in 1900).

The US went to war again in 1898. The Cuban people had arisen in revolt against its Spanish masters in 1895. In the US, the newspapers owned by William Randolph Hearst and Joseph Pulitzer were hungry for sensational and exiting news. The papers went into campaign mode and demanded that the US side with the freedom loving Cubans. Hearst sent an artist to Cuba to draw pictures of repression and humiliation. The artist reported that he found nothing of the kind. To which Hearst replied:

"You supply the drawings. I'll supply the war."

For the first but certainly not last time, media set the agenda. Since that time it has played a major role in US politics, not the least when it comes to foreign affairs.

The war went well. The Spaniards were routed and the US was now responsible for not only the island off the coast of Florida, but also the Philippines, Guam and Puerto Rico. It was, if reluctantly (and not for very long) a colonial power; Puerto Rico and Guam stayed American.

It was also, there can be no doubt about it, an empire, doomed to expand, reluctantly and without enthusiasm, but unstoppably. Even if it did not colonize Latin America, it made its will very well known and not always by diplomatic means. Indeed, as of this writing, the US has been militarily active south of the border no less than 32 times, in Nicaragua, Honduras, Panama, the Dominican Republic, and other countries.

Sweden, at the time of the Spanish-American war, had lost all its overseas possessions. The last one went away, not with a bang but with a whimper. It was the West Indian island of Saint Barthélemy, better known as St. Bart. Sweden bought it from France in 1784 and named the sleepy capital Gustavia after King Gustaf III. During the Napoleonic Wars the city profited mightily from its status as a free port, but when peace came things started to unravel. The Swedes really wanted to get rid of the place but were decent enough to arrange a referendum. The question was:

Do you wish to belong to Sweden or France?

Sweden got one vote, France all the rest.

In 1878 the little island changed hands. At that time Sweden had already become isolationistic and inward looking; after 1814 it would never go to war again. Increasingly the country played the role of spectator in international affairs, albeit a spectator that made its likes and dislikes very well known.

The colonization of the New World was only part of the great effort by the European powers, mainly Great Britain, France, Spain, Portugal, and to some extent the Netherlands and Germany, to conquer and rule as much of the world as possible. Colonialism, including the settlements in North America, started in earnest around 1500, after the discoveries made by the great seafarers from, mainly, the Iberian Peninsula.

Europeans discovered, conquered, and sometimes settled. They established trading posts and in time governments, administrations, and institutions. They also massacred, looted, raped, and cheated on every conceivable agreement. They were, after all, almost as chosen a people as the Americans. They had to, in Rudyard Kipling's eternal words, carry the white man's burden. They had to spread Christendom, in which they didn't succeed all to well, and civilize the savage people they encountered, in which they also didn't succeed particularly well.

Portugal took command over Latin America's giant, Brazil, as well as Angola on the west coast of Africa and Mozambique on the east coast. In 1602 the Dutch East India Company founded Batavia, Java, today Jakarta, Indonesia and capital for 220 million, mainly Muslims. France colonized parts of Canada (Quebec), but of course, the greatest empire of them all belonged to Queen Victoria of the UK. The largest of the possessions was India, including today's Pakistan, Singapore, Malaysia, Burma, Australia, and the Caribbean. India, often called 'the jewel in the crown', in time became the world's largest English speaking country, a fact of enormous importance later in history.

The Imperialists, including the Germans, divided Africa amongst them. Belgium's king, Leopold I, got Belgian Congo, about as large as Europe, as his personal possession, but the United Kingdom and France, of course, got much more. France took North Africa, minus the most important country, Egypt (which went to the UK), and Libya, which fell to the Italians. It also got a handful of countries in West and Central Africa. The UK took basically all the rest, including Rhodesia and the diamond and mineral rich area, which would become South Africa, and had to be taken over by force from the Boers, who were settlers of Dutch descent.

The colonies and dominions were of the utmost economic importance. In 1820 no less than 30 percent of world trade was tied to China and 15 percent to India. The US, which would 130 years later be totally dominant, represented only 2 percent.

The White Man saw to it that he was well paid for carrying that burden of his.

The surface of the United States is 9,631,420 km2 / 3,718,695 sq mi
Population density in the US is 31 per km2 / 80 per sq mi

The surface of Sweden is 449,964 km2 / 173,732 sq mi
In Sweden the population density is 20 per km2 / 52 per sq mi

With over 300 million inhabitants, the USA is 33 times as big as Sweden in population (Sweden: 9 million). Eight of the States are bigger than Sweden. The State of Minnesota, which attracted more Swedish immigrants than any other state has 4.9 million people. In surface, the US is 21 times as large as Sweden; the largest state, California, is equal in surface but has 4 times as many inhabitants.

Sweden's largest city, Stockholm (the capital) would rank 6th or 7th in the United States, where the largest city, New York, has almost as many inhabitants as all of Sweden.

3

Colonization, Wallenberg, and World Wars

Way before the word 'colonialism' came in use, that European Great Power, Sweden, had colonized, in its rude fashion, a large part of the Baltic countries and a not inconsiderable part of Central Europe. It seemed only natural that it should also try to take part in the colonizing of the New World, this in spite of the fact that money was a grave problem.

In 1639, some nineteen years after the Mayflower sailed, but only seven years after the death of Gustav II Adolf in the epic battle at Lützen, two Swedish ships, Calmare Nyckel and Fogel Grip arrived in Delaware. For financial and other reasons the expedition was a joint venture between Swedish and Dutch interests; the leader, Peter Minuit, was Dutch with the goal to found a colony. The settlers bought land from the local Indians and built a small fort, called Fort Christina, after the queen who was the daughter of the great Hero King (but later became a Catholic, abdicated, and went to live in Rome).

The Dutch were bought out in 1641, and the Swede Johan Printz, whom the Indians for good reasons called Big Gut, became governor. He was as energetic and enterprising as he was fat, but the colony, New Sweden, was no success. Conditions were harsh, enemies and competitors abounded. Farming went reasonably well, but no industry came into being and the people stayed poor. Attempts to lure more Swedes across the Atlantic failed, and in 1655 the Dutch forced the Swedes to cede the area.

It was roughly at that point in time when Sweden started to shrink in area, power, and status, a fact that not even well educated Swedes were aware of at the time.

It was still a country to be reckoned with through the Napoleonic Wars in the beginning of the 19th century, but less and less so. Even the death of Charles XII in 1718 had some influence, mainly because people were used to it having influence. Media in our sense of the word did not yet exist, and reality in those days changed faster than the perception of reality. That is most likely the reason Charles continued to fascinate people all over the world for a long, long time to come (more of which comes later in the story).

Maybe the fiasco in the New World was the reason very few Swedes immigrated to America before the USA existed. Actually there was no mass influx of Swedes until after the Civil War. Another reason certainly was that the New World was very, very far away. The trip was expensive and dangerous, and ordinary Swedes were poor, without knowledge of the world, fatigued by all the wars, and generally without ambition to do much more than scrape by.

To the few, the very few who knew something about America, it also became known as a dangerous place, where white and red people fought each other with great intensity and cruelty (just like the Europeans did and continued doing at home), and many people were slaves.

Slavery as a way of life was hardly anything new in Europe, including Sweden, and absolutely not in Russia, where the Czar owned all the small peasants, millions and millions of them. The life of a serf was valued as absolutely nothing, a peasant's not much more. True, Swedish peasants were never slaves in a formal way, but in spite of this, they were hard-pressed to pay steep taxes for all the wars as well as to send their sons to die in these wars.

In America, on the other hand, slavery very soon became formal and codified in law. The first slave ship from Africa landed in Jamestown, Virginia in 1619, a year before the Mayflower. The ship flew the Dutch flag and the captain exchanged his cargo for food. The trading of people had its origin in ancient times and had long been practiced by the Arabs; now it entered the New World were it was to become very big indeed.

Jamestown was the first British colony, founded in 1607 and named for King James I. Its first two years were disastrous. Of three hundred settlers, two hundred and forty died from diseases or from fighting the Indians (of whom there were between 1 and 12 million in all of North America; more precise figures don't exist). An entrepreneur by the name of John Rolfe, who managed to crossbreed tobacco from the West Indies with the later so famous Virginia, saved the colony. Within a decade Jamestown profited mightily from the export of tobacco.

The visit by the Dutch ship was the beginning of another much more profitable trade. Slave traders from many nations bought young men and women from chiefs in West Africa. In the 18th century some 100,000 were brought in every year. In return, the traders got more and more tobacco. The slaves were put to work in the fields and in the (increasingly stately) mansions. A black woman, at the time, cost 120 pounds (or some 55 kilos) of tobacco, a good worker a bit more. At first a slave was defined simply as a non-Christian, but later as a person with colored (i.e. black) skin. Needless to say, slavery spread from Jamestown to the other colonies, 13 to begin with (see next chapter).

Slavery was precisely that, slavery. As somebody has rightfully written: During a great deal of its history, the US enslaved and segregated blacks, massacred and marginalized Indians, discriminated against Catholics and made it difficult for immigrants that did not come from Northern Europe.

Not very nice. But true.

Segregation was total and taken as a matter of fact; there is absolutely no reason to believe that the early Swedes questioned or protested against this, as Sweden was very much a class society, where everybody was expected to know his place and behave accordingly.

A slave had no rights whatsoever, although many owners discovered that a good worker had to be fed reasonably well to function well, just like an engine has to be oiled and happy to perform well.

As Samuel P. Huntington has stated, America (the part today known as the USA) was founded in the 17th and 18th centuries by settlers, almost all of whom were Protestant, coming from the British Isles, mainly at the beginning of the Puritan strain. In short, while Martin Luther and John Calvin spearheaded Reformation on the European continent, none other than King Henry VIII, with his many wives, accomplished it in quite a different way in England. Royally mad at Pope Clement in Rome, who refused to annul a marriage of his (for reasons that have nothing to do with our story), Henry simply hijacked the Church. He then renamed it the Anglican Church and made himself its head. Eventually civil war ensued. After Oliver Cromwell's years of dictatorship, restoration of monarchy, and what has been called the Great Persecution, British Protestants came under heavy pressure and many fled to America, where they founded the colonies. Among the first were the Quakers, led by William Penn, founder of Pennsylvania, but the majority settled in New England.

The settlers should not be confused with immigrants. They came to create a new order, to build new cities and form a new culture, not, like later day immigrants, to adjust to an already existing system. They came to conquer, not to fit in.

The people who would settle in America came first from England, then from other parts of Great Britain, then Germany and Holland. At the time of the Declaration of Independence in 1776, 80 percent of the US population came from Britain, the rest from Germany and Holland. No less than 98 percent were Protestant, and equally important, because having been persecuted and more or less forced to flee, very strong in their beliefs.

Belief in God was strong even among the people they left behind in Europe, but that would change. Today, a bit more than 200 years later, the US is as Christian (still mainly Protestant) as ever. Europe, on the other hand, is populated almost totally by nonbelievers: A fact of enormous consequence and one of the main reasons the two continents drifted so widely apart after the break up of the Soviet Union in 1991. (Up to that time what was called the Atlantic Bloc was held together by fear of Communism.)

Sweden might in fact be the least religious country in the Europe of today. Young people see Christendom as a slightly ridiculous kind of superstition and consider fundamentalists (including President George W. Bush) as more or less madmen. But more on this subject later in the book.

As already said, immigrants are prepared to change their ways, at least to some degree, to conform. Settlers on the other hand come to create a new society, to sculpt the new land according to their wishes. Having fought wars and suffered all kinds of persecution, the European Protestants were not going to let anybody, let alone the heathen redskins, stand in their way.

In part because of this, the Indian War of 1675-76 became the bloodiest in the country's history. On a proportional basis, twice as many settlers lost their lives as were lost in the Civil War and seven times as many as in WWII. Many years later it all ended with the Native Americans being more or less extinct, the remaining minority living on reservations (often supported by gambling casinos) and playing no great role in the nation's business.

It should be noted that 1) the men killing the Indians were, as stated earlier, all Europeans, a fact all too often forgotten today, when the genocidal massacres are blamed on "the Americans," and 2) the proportion of Christians in the US is greater than that of Jews in Israel, Muslims in

Egypt, or Hindus in India.

As Huntington states, the US became a nation in part because the former colonists had enemies to fight: England, France, and the Indians. Not to mention each other, when the Civil War came.

Few Swedes set out for the New World before the Civil War. But then, they came in droves.

Emigration in great numbers started around 1865. The mass exodus continued up to 1914, driven mainly by bad harvests, hunger, and poverty. Between those years more than a million Swedes crossed the Atlantic, the overwhelming majority never to come back. At one time, one million Swedes made up some 20 percent of the population, which means that, proportionally, very few countries gave as generously of its youth to America. In some areas, like my home province of Halland, more than half the population left, the great majority of the emigrants being between 15 and 35 years of age. The largest single group consisted of second sons of poor farmers—the oldest son inherited the farm, the second was all too often penniless.

But free to leave.

The two countries were, of course, not alike, but in one important sense they were. Both were mainly agricultural. The Swedes who left were poor farmers or even poorer farmhands. They left a country were they felt un-free and downtrodden, and they landed in one where they were free to do what they wished; they got more soil to till than they had ever dreamed of— almost for free. They knew that they would have to work hard and were eager to do it, not the least because here, they would be working for themselves. They saw dizzyingly great fields and forests that were suddenly *their own* and felt that surge of optimism which is (even today) America's greatest gift to humanity.

The Swedes were almost all Lutheran Christians. They had grown up learning to work hard, obey the law, and even more so to obey their teachers, priests, bosses, and employers, who, all too often were a law unto themselves. From this, they broke up, quite determined never to be downtrodden again. In his famous epic "*Invandrarna*", (The Immigrants) author Wilhelm Moberg writes:

"The disobedient folks from the old world were young people. Three fourths of the population in the Minnesota Territories consisted of people less than 30 years of age. There were no feeble oldsters to support. The immigrants were young people in a young land... For them life began

41

anew: they had to rely totally on themselves and could use their strengths freely… And here nobody felt class or rank, here nobody possessed inherited rights or advantages… Everyone was valued according his skills… The land was great beyond measure and with the country their dreams grew…"

Nobody stood in the way any longer. They were free at last. In fact, each and every Swede or German or Pole or Englishman who set out for the country on the other side of the Atlantic made a private declaration of independence from the old country. Each and everyone became an American even before there was an American state. This, more than anything else, made it inevitable that an independent state would follow and that it would continue to be the land of choice for independent minded men and women from all over the world.

The US became —and still is—*the* country of choice, and those who made the choice almost inevitably committed themselves fully to the new nation.

Many of the emigrants were woefully undereducated; my grandfather, born 1870, who spent some time in the US, had hardly gone to school at all; my father, born as late as 1891, had all of five years of education, sometimes interrupted when sand from dunes along the sea in Halland blew in and blocked the road. Many could hardly read or write, almost all were dirt poor to the degree that they had actually starved or at the very least gone hungry for days and weeks.

Not unnaturally, they had come to detest their country of birth as authoritarian and closed, if not a prison, certainly not a place where a poor man was really free. Wealth belonged to a few who were not eager to share it, and who were, common folks felt, protected by law, police, and all other instruments of power. A song, popular for decades, stated that the thing to do was to go to the big country in the west, where there is no king and no intrusive priests, and (maybe even more important) where for dinner you can eat pork and potatoes and then use the grease to polish your boots "all gratis."

It should be added that many decided to run because they didn't want to be drafted into the army or navy; to fight and die for Sweden had been an honorable, even noble option in earlier centuries but no more.

In America, which had always been a relatively classless society even before 1776, the immigrants, including the Swedes, for the first time in their lives found equality. Any man was as worthy as the next man and nobody stood in the way if you were ready to work hard to better your lot. To a large extent this is still true in spite of the fact that poverty persists and large groups, mainly Latinos, have a tougher time of it.

It is also true that Sweden also started to change in a positive direction. There was a change in approach to and construction of a system that mandated not equality of opportunity but a kind of mechanical equality through equal income after taxes - from cradle to grave and regardless of personal effort.

This strange system will be further explored in coming chapters.

In 1800, when the long period of war, war, war, was at last over, only two Swedish cities, Stockholm and Gothenburg, had more than 10,000 inhabitants. But now, growth took off. Between 1800 and 1900 the population more than doubled from 2.4 to 5.4 million. Particularly after 1870 when industrialization started in earnest, people began moving from the countryside to the urban areas, seeking jobs in industry rather than staying down on the farm. In 1900, the proportion of people working in agriculture had shrunk from 90 percent to 50; almost 30 percent were industrial workers. The Social Democratic Party, founded in 1889, and also called the Workers' Party, was in a good position to profit from this.

During the highly expansive period leading up to the First World War, Sweden built railways and a lot of great industrial enterprises. Lars Magnus Ericsson created the telephone company that bears his name, today a world leader. We saw the birth of Separator, Bolinders, Asea (the Swedish part of ABB), some of the world's leading shipyards and a forest industry that produced paper for, among others, leading newspapers like *The Times* of London and *Le Figaro* in Paris. Among those companies, the most prominent was Stora Kopparbergs Bergslags AB, the world's oldest shareholding company. (Once in the 1960's, Stora applied for a loan from Chase Manhattan Bank. The bank for some reason demanded a more detailed presentation. When Stora commenced this presentation by stating that it was the oldest existing company, the loan was immediately granted.)

Alfred Nobel invented (in 1875) what became dynamite and gathered one of the world's largest fortunes. After his death, this fortune was donated to the foundation, which pays the very prestigious Nobel prizes, which bring Sweden into media focus all over the world each December.

All the great financial and industrialist families mentioned above were to disappear except one: the Wallenbergs. The US economy has created enormously powerful families like the Rockefellers, the Carnegies, the

Mellons, the Fords and many others, but because of the country's size and diversity, none of them has had anything like the influence of the Wallenbergs in Sweden. Indeed, the family was for many years a state within the state, extremely powerful in domestic affairs and by far better connected in international power centers than the government, something that played a very important role during WWII and the Cold War. Wallenberg is the name you'll find most often in the pages of this book; here is how they started.

Stockholms Enskilda Bank, predecessor of SEB (Skandinaviska Enskilda Banken), owned and run by the family, was established in 1856, even before the Social Democratic Party, which was founded in 1889. The founder, marine captain André Oscar Wallenberg was quite a character. He commanded the country's first propeller driven ship, the steamer Linköping, which connected Stockholm with Linköping via the relatively recently completed Göta Kanal—the man-made channel connecting Sweden's west coast with the Baltic. One crewmember was 18 year old Catharina Wilhelmina Andersson, poor and fatherless, but very beautiful. The captain and the cleaning girl fell in love and "Mina" eventually gave birth to five children of whom three survived. One survivor was Knut W. who became chief of the bank and for a few years foreign minister—he was at that time so rich that the fact that he was born out of wedlock was not held against him.

It was many years before André Oscar's mother, a bishop's widow, gave permission for AO to marry. Mina then had one legitimate son, but she died shortly after his birth. Her place in the stately home was taken over by her older sister Lovisa, with whom AO fathered two children. However, after he founded the bank it was decided that he must marry somebody from his own social class, so Lovisa had to go. Instead Wallenberg married Anna von Sydow, who gave birth to no less than fourteen children, among them Marcus W. the Elder, perhaps the greatest empire builder in Sweden's industrial and financial history.

The reason I am revealing the details of AO Wallenberg's private life is that they were kept secret for the general public for more than 150 years, just like Prime Minister Per Albin Hansson's bigamy was covered up for many decades. The reasons were that one simply doesn't talk about such matters in Sweden. Whispered gossip was allowed (if primarily in inside circles) but no newspaper editor worth his salt would even dream of scandalizing a fine family or a prominent politician. Ordinary people would have protested loudly. And besides: Who needs enemies as powerful as the Wallenbergs?

The family indeed became steadily more powerful as time went by.

The year the bank was founded was the year the first railways were built, opening the country and creating opportunities for timber merchants, ironwork entrepreneurs, and soon a host of brilliant inventors.

The Wallenbergs were quick to realize the importance of the railways. Around the time when Per Albin made his speech about the people's home, the family was already known all over the country. The leading member was Judge Marcus Wallenberg, Sr., who besides the bank controlled (among others) the following companies, some of them of world class:

> Stora Kopparbergs Bergslags AB.
>
> SKF (the world's leading ball bearing concern).
>
> Stockholm-Westerås-Bergslagen Railway.
>
> Halmstad-Nässjö Railway.
>
> Wifstavarf (a famous steel works).

Later on the empire would add ASEA (founded 1883, famous for a power transmission, automation, nuclear reactors, etc), Ericsson (telephones), Electrolux (vacuum cleaners, refrigerators), Bofors (weapons), and much, much more to its holdings. It is fair to say that the majority of Per Albin's followers, thousands and thousands of them, worked for the Wallenbergs, quite often at machines that had earlier been manned by their dads or grand dads, always unprotected against arbitrary dismissal and unemployment, almost always paid salaries that only barely kept body and soul together.

In the 1910's, Judge Marcus Wallenberg's brother Knut, who had no children, established the Knut and Alice Wallenberg Foundation, to which he willed the better part of his considerable wealth. The dividends paid to the Foundation are converted to grants to various research projects. Nobody denies that the money has been well spent, but much more important is the fact that the Foundation is tax exempt and therefore able to preserve the family's control of the many companies decade after decade.

If Knut and Alice Wallenberg had had children who had inherited all the shares, Sweden would likely have been a very different country, a bewildering reminder of how coincidences can form history. As it were, the Foundation's giant holdings became a major power center and have so remained. Indeed, one could say that no other institution in the country has played the same role when it comes to keep overwhelming financial power within the same family generation after generation. It stands to reason that if the Social Democrats had wanted to break the family's hold on power without going for socialization in general, one could have changed the laws governing the taxation of foundations so much more so as the making and changing of laws soon became a specialty.

Nothing of that kind happened. Per Albin left power to Tage Erlander, who was succeeded by Palme, who was succeeded by Ingvar Carlsson, who was succeeded by Göran Persson. All five were strong prime ministers, yet the most powerful man in Swedish industry (and possibly in the country) was always named Wallenberg. As already stated, the family will appear in yet more pages of the book. Here, two important observations are enough:

1. Capitalism, personified by the Wallenberg family, was a power in Sweden long before the Social Democratic Party. Even if the party was founded as early as 1889, many years passed before it gained real power; the same goes for the trade union's central organization, the LO, founded in 1898. No Swedish political leader has had the slightest chance to compete with the Wallenbergs for influence and control without opposition and in real time over the country's most important companies. Rather there have been two parallel governments that have given Sweden one Capitalist ruling class and one Socialist, not necessarily fond of each other but committed to cooperate as efficiently and rationally (treasured qualities in Sweden) as possible... but in secret and over the heads of common folks.

2. At the time the Social Democrats started their march to power, the companies were still very Swedish and the owners were firmly convinced that they should remain so. In many company bylaws foreign ownership was outright prohibited. Also, a graduated voting right made it very hard even for domestic hopefuls, and there were never many to challenge the Wallenbergs. Of at least equal interest is the fact that several of the heavyweights in the Social Democratic Party worked hand in glove with the Empire. Shortly before he died, Vice Premier Odd Engström revealed how, late one Thursday night each month, he used to open the door to the finance ministry to let in Marcus Wallenberg, Jr., who came to see Finance Minister Gunnar Sträng. The two powerful men spoke the same language and arranged things to their liking, of course without witnesses, protocol, or written agreements. In spite of the fact that this happened during the revolutionary 1970's, both men were contemptuous of media and absolutely convinced that democratic transparency is impractical and unnecessary, not to say disruptive.

"Here comes the chief of the private sector," Sträng joked on one occasion when Wallenberg entered a reception. Everybody found it charming and very, very Swedish, but more about that later.

Before 1914 Europe led a quite happy life. Backed by a common gold standard, money flowed freely between the countries. You did not need a passport to travel and could get a job anywhere (if you spoke the language half well). In Sweden the State Church was very powerful, and the free congregations as well as the Temperance Movement were much larger than the political parties. Marriage outside the Church was not allowed until 1908, and an up and coming Social Democrat by the name of Per Albin Hansson, later to be the father of the country, believed that prohibition of alcohol ought to be written into the party's program. He also believed in unilateral disarmament.

I might add that Per Albin, as earlier mentioned, was in reality married to two women at the same time. The press knew it, but at the time one didn't reveal private matters to the general public. In this respect, media in Sweden and the US for a long time played by the same rules. Neither newspapers nor radio nor TV in the US said a word about the manifold entanglements of FDR and JFK.

The first great leader of the Social Democratic Party was not Per Albin, who had a working class background, but the aristocratic Hjalmar Branting. He started out as a convinced Marxist and accepted that the inevitable impoverishment of the masses would lead to revolution. However, he relatively soon began to think along more reformist lines. The right to vote more and more became the key issue in Swedish politics, gradually convincing even one-time revolution enthusiasts like Per Albin and Gustaf Möller that a bloody upheaval would not be needed.

Reform, however, was long in coming. While men in France got the right to vote in 1848, Sweden waited until 1866. Even then the right was restricted to men with a yearly income of 800 riksdaler, much more than a worker could make, or an ownership of real estate valued at 1,000 riksdaler, which was also out of reach. All in all, 21 percent of the men could vote, but, of course no women. The Liberal Party, which was leading the movement, demanded more, and with the help of the Social Democrats finally succeeded in achieving one man, one vote in 1907, overcoming many years of stiff resistance by the Conservatives under Admiral (and Prime Minister) Arvid Lindman. Women were not allowed to vote until 1918.

Very few, if any, American and Swedish politicians exchanged views during the years up to and through the First World Ward. In the US, Presidents Theodore Roosevelt (Republican 1901-09) and Woodrow Wilson (Democrat 1913-21), were regarded as progressives who tried to fight corporate abuse by busting trusts, introducing a federal income tax, establishing the Federal Reserve Board, and generally trying to make life easier for working families.

In Sweden, Branting and his followers managed to push through laws for workers' protection, and more importantly, a general pension insurance (in 1913).

When the First World War started in the summer of 1914 with that fateful shot in Sarajevo, Sweden had long since decided to stay neutral. The US, which had been to war only 14 years earlier, was in an isolationistic period, and President Wilson immediately issued a proclamation of neutrality. His decision was no doubt popular with the great majority of the people, weary of entangling alliances and opposed to war, even if most Americans, not unnaturally, favored Great Britain and France.

Sweden kept neutral all through the war in spite of having its ports blockaded by both sides in the conflict. As for the US, everything changed when in 1917 German torpedoes sank six American ships. Congress passed a war resolution and Woodrow Wilson proclaimed that:

"The world must be made safe for democracy ...we have no selfish ends to serve. We desire no conquest, no dominion."

The US threw its considerable resources into the war and, as we know, prevailed. The war needs not to be described in this book. It is, however, of the greatest importance that we note the four most important consequences of the war to end all wars, making the world safe for democracy:

1.   The Swedish Social Democratic Youth League donated 300 crowns to Vladimir Illitj Lenin. Leftists in Sweden, like many other countries, had read Karl Marx and dreamed of a workers and peasants state without czars and noble men. More important is, of course, that the leader of the Russian Communists got ample financing from Germany as well as the right to go by train through Germany, Sweden, and Finland, on his way to St. Petersburg and his rendezvous with history. The war had sapped Russia's strength. The Czar was finished and the Bolsheviks eventually took power, meaning torture and death for millions of people and enslavement for hundreds of millions. As early as December 22, 1917, the party organ, *Social-Demokraten* wrote in a leading article: "the Russian Bolsheviks murder democracy... supported by armed might, a minority abolishes representative government." The OP-ED leader was most likely written by Per Albin Hansson.

At the same time, we should note that some historians think that there was a real possibility for revolution in Sweden, too. The war made the food situation in Sweden precarious, not the least because of a very profitable export to Germany. The blame fell on two conservatives, Hjalmar Hammarskjöld (Dag Hammskjöld's dad, who was called *hunger-skjöld*) and Carl Swartz, and the country was for many weeks quite tense. However, because of the calm and reasonableness of Branting and the other Social Democratic leaders, the situation was kept in check. Two cabinet ministers during the war, ship owners Dan Broström and K. A. Wallenberg, made millions by supplying Germany with goods blockaded by Great Britain; their feat was to be repeated by many others, but particularly by the Wallenberg family, during the next world war.

2.   The war ended with the disastrous peace in Versailles outside of Paris. The Germans were forced to accept terms - including enormous war reparations that were insulting and in the end disastrous. The result was general dissatisfaction, with galloping inflation, the destruction of the middle class, and in the end, Adolf Hitler and the Nazis.

3.   The League of Nations was in no small measure created by Woodrow Wilson, perhaps the most idealistic president the US has ever had. Wilson saw the organization as a means to facilitate the settlement of disputes between the states, a more or less continuously ongoing negotiation where small nations would have a good chance of getting allies and protection from more powerful and aggressive neighbors. In other words: A world where calm and reason ruled. Hjalmar Branting, who eventually became one of the leading statesmen in the League, was believer from day one. From the very outset Sweden made a firm commitment to conflict resolution through what was later called the International Community. So did many other small nations but very few have kept up the commitment as fervently as Sweden.

4.   The US, however, was not a small state. Neither was it weak. It had just won the greatest war in history. At the same time, all other Great Powers had lost: Germany and Russia outright, the UK and France in so far as they had both lost a generation of young men, and in the case of France, suffered massive material destruction. Europe, to cut it short, was finished, while the US was well on its way to becoming a super power.

A super power does not want its hands tied, and in spite of Woodrow Wilson's commitment, the Senate refused to ratify US membership in the League of Nations. The most important geopolitical consequence of this was that the US left the European continent, where it would have been one of the strongest powers, had it chosen to stay. If it had stayed engaged as it did after the Second World War, it would have had a much greater chance of blocking Hitler and changing the course of history. It is perhaps an exaggeration to say that the US failed or abandoned Europe as in fact Sweden did during the Cold War. Yet, it is fair to say that had the Americans chosen to throw their weight around a little more after Versailles, the world would have looked quite different today.

And most likely much, much better, if you ask me.

Economic growth per capita

If we make the rather absurd hypothetical experiment and envision a USA entirely without growth between 2000 and 2005, while the economies in Europe kept growing with a normal pace, only one nation would even come close to the USA, in terms of GNP growth per capita. That country is Ireland; Sweden would still be left behind with at least $10,000 per capita.

Source: "EU versus USA" by Fredrik Bergström and Robert Gidehag.

4

State monopoly, the Mafia
(and quite a few other things!)

The word *Folkhemmet* was first used by Per-Albin Hansson on a beautiful summer evening in 1921. The term loses a lot in translation. Literally it means the People's Home, but what it really suggests is a great tent for everybody, the great society. It is a country where the citizens, all for one and one for all, look after each other, like the members of a good and loving family, where the head, which is the Government, decides what is good for everybody. As far as anyone knows, the word was the brainchild of a now forgotten politician in the Farmers' Party, which was conservative (in the very cautious, Swedish way), but Per Albin and his supporters quickly hijacked it. Some time after that first use, already the undisputed leader went on to wrap himself in the flag, saying:

"People have often said of us Social Democrats that we have no fatherland. But I say: there is no more patriotic party than the Social Democratic, in as much as the greatest patriotic achievement is to so develop our country that each and every citizen feels that he has a home here. IN THE GREAT HOME THERE SHALL NOT BE STEPCHILDREN NOR PETCHILDREN..."

No modern, political consultant, I dare say, could have come up with a better sales pitch, appealing to patriotism and equality at the same time, and this from the voice of a man in a rumpled suit and a little potbelly, a man easy to identify with.

Interestingly, in view of later events, Per Albin added:

"Do you think that so many of our best youth would have gone to America if this had been a just society...?"

Indeed, even before the war, in 1930 Sweden became, for the first time in many decades, a country importing, rather than exporting people. It has remained so ever since, although there are signs that the trend might one day be broken - more and more citizens want out nowadays, particularly to the USA. But to that, we shall return.

The time between the wars saw Sweden looking more and more inward, more and more determined to make life better for all Swedes, but particularly for the new class of industrial workers and the growing mass of functionaries. The stress was on protecting the people, teaching them to live according to rules set by various experts and to build machinery that would stop people from making mistakes or, when this failed, correct the mistakes. More and more the authorities, in Sweden called The Common (*det allmänna*), were in command, not the individuals.

A few years stand out:

In 1917 the selling of liquor was made a state monopoly. A rationing system was implemented, which gave a grown man the right to buy 1 liter of strong spirits per month. More affluent folks could get up to 3 liters. The sale was registered in a booklet (called *Motboken*) and duly stamped. At special occasions like weddings, funerals, or 50th birthdays, one could apply for a larger ration and probably receive it. If somebody became known as a drunk, the Motbok could be confiscated. People who had the book but didn't drink alcohol themselves did of course sell their aquavit. This was unlawful but impossible to stop. The system became known as "The System," and all liquor stores carried that name, which is still in use. The stores werenot (and are still not) allowed to advertise their wares; to display bottles in the windows is prohibited. The somewhat impossible ambition is to sell liquor, and since the booze is so heavily taxed, rake in money for the state, and simultaneously discourage people from touching the stuff.

Similar restrictions applied to the selling of liquor in restaurants. As a rule you could have three drinks of 5 centiliters each, usually two vodkas and one cognac, a ration known as "two white and one brown" because of the colors. For drinkers being the way they are, it soon became customary to invite a nondrinker to dinner in town. He or she got the food, the drinker the drink. I should know, for I lowered my food costs considerably by eating for free with a bunch of happy drinkers during a year as a young (and badly paid) journalist in the city of Varberg, Sweden.

As far as quantity of liquor is concerned, the restrictions were lifted in the fall of 1955, in spite of dire warnings that the country would soon drink itself to death, which did not happen. However, as already stated, the monopoly remained, becoming more and more ridiculous when people got more affluent and more mobile, going across the Öresund to more liberal Denmark to buy sometimes fantastic quantities of beer as well as stronger stuff. The situation for the monopoly got even worse, if that's the word you like to use, after Sweden became a member of the European Union in 1995. According to EU rules, free trade means FREE tradeand the French, Italian, and Spanish wine merchants, a mighty political lobby indeed, see to it that the rules are not broken. Sweden was allowed to restrict imports for a couple of years, but since then more and more people buy liquor in Denmark or Germany and buy by the truckloads.

The System is losing money in southern Sweden and might soon enough be close to collapse. A strong contributing factor is, in this field as in so many others, the high Swedish taxes. To make people drink less, the tax weapon makes liquor prohibitively expensive, and as a consequence a drink probably costs more in Sweden than in any other country, contributing to smuggling, legal buying abroad, and production of moonshine.The reason for the rationing was, of course, a wish shared by Per Albin Hansson (who did NOT say no to a drink) and many other politicians, to save the members of the people's home from themselves. Daddy knows best, would be an ever-recurring theme in Swedish life for decades and decades; indeed it still is. Quite naturally, defenders of the system are positive that they have succeeded, but no credible evidence exists. In the US, the UK, and all the countries on the European continent, liquor is more easily available than in Sweden. Yet, there is no sign that Danes, Frenchmen, or Britons are drinking themselves to death.

What the Swedes tried to do with rations and high taxes, the Americans tried to do with outright prohibition. Maine, Massachusetts, and a few other states were dry quite early, but it was after the First World War that the Temperance movement, strongly influenced by religious groups hoping to shape the perfect man, took off in earnest. During the war the production and sale of liquor was banned for some time to save grain, but it wasn't until 1919 that Congress passed the Volstead Act (named for Congressman Andrew J. Volstead), that in effect made drinking alcoholic beverages illegal.

Prohibition was at best a mixed success from the legislators' view. In the countryside, particularly in profoundly Christian areas, the law was followed, if mainly because people would not have been drinking anyway. In the big cities there were plenty of speak easies and other watering holes; bootleg liquor was available to anybody with money.

The Swedish idea that the sale of liquor should be undertaken by a monopoly was almost copied by one enterprising American. His name: Al Capone. Towards the end of the roaring twenties, Capone had killed and threatened his way to total dominance in the market. It is said that he turned over some 60 million dollars per year, a giant sum in those days, and had to share the loot with the taxman only late in his career. So, Sweden got a state monopoly, the US got the Mafia, both strongly dependent on alcohol. In Sweden, the state is still quite dependent on the use of alcohol, which it disingenuously pretends to control, of course, for the best of the people. In the US, development took a different route.

In 1933 Congress decided to repeal the Volstead Act. One of the businessmen who was well connected politically and ready to take advantage of the new situation was named Joseph Kennedy, father of Joe, Jr., JFK, Bobby, and Teddy. Kennedy imported whiskey from Scotland and was well stocked when the trade passed from the Mafia to legitimate establishments. So, it was a fortune largely based on alcohol that helped elect the US president who is perhaps the most admired in Sweden, as well as in the rest of Europe.

The second year to note is 1922.

That year Sweden got an institute for Racial Biology in Uppsala. What it was to do was simply keep the race clean. As leading politician and ideologist Arthur Engberg wrote:

"We have the good fortune to belong to a race that is so far relatively unspoiled, a race that is the bearer of very high and very good qualities. But the strange thing is that when we are very keen on pedigrees of our dogs and horses, we are not at all keen on looking at how we should preserve and protect our own Swedish stock. It is really about time that we do that."

In its first year, the institute measured the heads of 200,000 citizens to decide the shapes of the skulls of intelligent and dimwitted folks, respectively. That same year, Ernst Wigforss, one of the Social Democratic Party icons, proposed that one should improve the stock by sterilizing inferior human beings. The word he used was undermåliga, whichis pretty close to Hitler's "untermenschen," and not by chance. A bright and productive human being was useful and therefore good. A stupid and handicapped man or woman was not useful, therefore... well, not so good.

The Swedish laws about sterilization were second only to the laws in Nazi Germany. Exactly like the Germans, the Swedish leaders wanted to see tall and strong, blond and blue eyed people around them. The sick or handicapped or weak should be eliminated, not by slaughter - that would be inhumane - but gradually by being prohibited from breeding and producing new generations of defected and inferior people.

In the US during the same decades, black people and Native Americans were certainly not credited with the same human qualities as white folks. Racism there was. In Sweden, the discrimination hit mainly Swedish people since there were hardly any others at the time. Toa large degree the mentally handicapped and those thought to be mentally handicapped were singled out. In 1934 the laws were strengthened so that inferior and unfit women could be sterilized even against their will, and in 1941 it was also possible to sterilize people who conducted themselves in an asocial way—certainly a very broad definition.

The program quickly took off. All over the country the authorities, often local politicians (who worked ordinary jobs in the day time) found unfit and under-performing women: 95 percent of all persons sterilized were women that were deemed unworthy of having children. The women nearly always said yes to the operation, if only because they felt they had no other choice. Male juvenile delinquents were routinely sterilized before being sent out to help with the harvest in the summertime. That way there was no risk that they would leave behind unwanted and (of course!) inferior offspring.

In 1945 1,747 Swedes were sterilized, in 1947 no fewer than 2,264—or six per day. Rumor has it that the tempo was increased because one was concerned that the unfit (and then their more inferior children) would cost too much when parents were paid a subsidy for each child, a program that began in 1948 (and still goes on, the principle being that everybody, even billionaires, should be included).

In 1945, Hitler's extermination camps had been known for three years and the persecution of the racially unfit Jews known considerably longer. Towards the end of 1945, Auschwitz and other camps were opened for the media, but in Sweden sterilization continued. Why?

How could men like Per Albin, Gustaf Möller, and Tage Erlander condone, indeed order, this shockingly undemocratic, cruel, and unfair program?

The answer is quite simple. They really thought that by eliminating the inferior unborn, a cleaner, healthier race would gradually be produced. Human life could and should be engineered, of course by the elite. By stopping poor Elsa, the not so bright servant girl who already had two children with different fathers, from having a third baby, one did good. Good to Elsa, in spite of her tears, and good to society, too.

I should know. My mother was in charge of the program in our little village in the 1940's. As a boy, I now and then sat at her side at the kitchen table when she convinced a young woman to forgo children forever. Mom was convinced she did a good deed, the rational thing. So, at the time, was I. We belonged to the workers movement. We wanted to create a new world, where inferior people simply didn't exist.

I should add that similar thoughts existed all around the world, the difference being that it was easier to bring about action in a small, rather isolated and extremely homogenous country like Sweden.

Today it's easy to say that the sterilization program was social engineering run wild. But in the 1930's, social engineering was much in demand and the absolutely most important members of the corps of engineers were the Myrdals, Gunnar and Alva. Gunnar was to become world famous for his monumental study of race in the US, "An American Dilemma," still a must read for anybody interested in the subject. He eventually got a Nobel Prize in economics and was widely considered a genius. Alva was not a genius but generally thought of as clearheaded and thinking along the right lines, particularly if you think that society should be an organism devoted to hygiene, efficiency, discipline, and productivity. In the world according to Alva Myrdal, the citizens, well at least the ordinary ones, should exist to serve the state (called the common good), not the other way around. The individual's goal in life should be to produce and conform. For dissenters or rebels there should be no room.

In a famous study of the social engineers, author Yvonne Hirdman writes: "The State represented everybody, represented a higher consciousness than common consciousness… well arranged was the same as the planned, and the planned was the efficient. Behind democracy as the proclaimed, ultimate goal stood efficiency as the unspoken, even higher goal."

With cold contempt, Hirdman notes that the social engineers wanted to control ordinary folks' lives down to the smallest details while being themselves the ruling elite and therefore free to do whatever they liked. In 1934, the Myrdals published a truly frightening book titled *"Kris i befolkningsfrågan"* (Crisis in the Population Issue) in which the authors claimed expertise in sexual issues as well as the upbringing of children (something their son Jan, a well known writer, hatefully denied many years later). The background to the study was that Sweden's demography didn't look right. For the foreseeable future there were too few Swedes for the large scale, centralistic project the social engineers were burning to kick-start. The solution one envisaged was to produce more Swedes.

More and of higher quality. (Because sterilization gradually eliminated the inferior and unfit). The Myrdals wanted to make the upbringing of children a collective enterprise, to legislate rules for where people were to live, what they were to eat, and what clothes they were to wear. All children would be registered at school so that the authorities knew everything about parents, size of home, number of siblings, etc.

Luckily, in spite of the fame of the engineers, the politicians did not bite, at least not initially and not to the extent the authors wished. The reason was that the war came and consumed the resources. The attempts to collectivize Swedish society returned later. Tragically, they succeeded all too well (more of this later).

The 1930's was a time of strong men, like Hitler in Germany, Mussolini in Italy, Pilsudski in Poland, Ataturk in Turkey, Dolfuss in Austria, Horthy in Hungary, Masaryk in Czechoslovakia and, yes, Franklin Roosevelt in the US, and Per Albin Hansson in Sweden.

At the time of the Great Depression what the strong men did in the US and Sweden did not differ so much. In his irrepressible optimism, Roosevelt claimed, "the only thing we have to fear is fear itself." The banks were closed but only to open as soon as possible. The Federal Emergency Relief Act gave the states money and the Agricultural Adjustment Administration transferred funds to needy farmers (of whom there were millions). The Social Security Act established old age pensions and unemployment compensation was instituted. In short, a safety net was established, in the US as well as in Sweden. The difference, which is fundamental, is this:

In the US it was always clear that as far as it was possible, the individual should work and support himself and the people dependent on him. When times got difficult, there would be help, but it would be limited to what was absolutely necessary. It cannot be stressed too strongly that the responsibility rested on the individual. In Sweden, as I have shown above, the social engineers and their political counterparts wanted to create, not a temporary, but a permanent system, the all encompassing welfare state. It was clearly understood that the ordinary Swede was and should always be a part of a collective, governed from above. Per Albin himself, undisputed party leader after Branting's death in 1925, quite soon came to think that Sweden ought to be ruled foreverby a coalition government where decisions would be taken by consensus. That he saw himself as the leader of that government, there is no question. And as coming chapters will show, it almost turned out that way.

It remains to be said that the 1932 death of Match King Ivar Kreuger hit the Swedish bourgeoisie very hard. Kreuger had concentrated in his concern almost all match production in the world. He became so rich that he could give loans not only to individuals and companies but indeed to states, like Italy, Romania, and others. He was, wrote famed economist John Kenneth Galbraith, the Marshall planner of his time (after the first Great War) and considered perhaps the world's leading financier. However, many of his deals turned sour with the Depression, and at last the secretive, devious, and possibly criminal man saw no other way out than to shoot himself. (To this day, hundreds of conspiracy buffs believe that he was murdered; dozens of books to that effect exist.) Kreuger's death sapped the strength of Sweden's business elite with the notable exception of the Wallenberg family, which took over the best part of Kreuger's empire (at very favorable prices) and further allied itself with the Social Democrats, who in precisely that year formed the government we still have.

The third year of note is 1925.

That was the year *Radiotjänst* (literally Radioservice) was founded. Again, the state took monopoly on the distribution of news and entertainment via the airwaves. Again, the purpose was the same as when the sale of alcohol was restricted. Ordinary people should not be trusted. They might prefer bawdy and unclean entertainment, fall prey to commercial tricks, and so on (commercial being a deeply derogatory term in Sweden to this day). Worse still, if the distribution of news was not handled responsibly, sensational and untrue stories might make the poor, uneducated souls upset.

All this protection, of course, was (and is) pure hypocrisy. As the future clearly shows, the name of the game was control of news and therefore of opinion. When television made its debut in the mid 1950's, it was taken for granted that it would develop as a parallel monopoly; indeed for a long time radio and TV worked under the same CEO and the same board, all in practice, if not formally, picked by the government.

In fact, the Social Democrats were always scared out of their wits when confronted with commercial TV. The US and the UK got television in the late 1940's, France 1950, Holland '51, Germany '52, Belgium, Switzerland, and Japan '53, Denmark and Ireland '54. Sweden, untouched by the war and in possession of a quite efficient electronic industry, could indeed have been in the forefront of the development but chose not to be. None other than Olof Palme best formulated the reason. Quoted in a book written by his admirer Björn Elmbrant, he said:

"I would in all humility like to state that among the years of my life best used in the public service were (the years) I devoted to fight the thought of commercializing Swedish radio and television."

In an interview with a French journalist, Palme was even more explicit:

"To offer these means of communication to advertising, to the auctioning out of consumer products...that is a sneaky way of slowing the development of the individual, that is to sacrifice the power of individuals for the power of money..."

Palme and his admirers, who were many and included the intellectual elite of the country, were adamant in their belief that advertising made products more expensive; competition and freedom of choice simply didn't enter into the equation. Some of the supporters, indeed, went even further than Palme. In 1980 (note the year!) Maj-Britt Theorin, a Social Democratic member of parliament asked for a ban on parabolic antennas that can catch foreign programs that could hurt children and undereducated people. How it would hurt, she did not explain. Neither did she, nor Palme, nor any other prominent Social Democrat confess to the obvious: they wanted to continue to have control over the media, particularly television.

No wonder it took until the very end of 1987 for Sweden to get commercial TV. Swedish entrepreneur Jan Stenbeck, scion of a well-known finance family but operating out of New York, had found a loophole in the law. If a commercial telecast beamed by satellite was directed not only to Sweden, but also to all of Scandinavia, it did not come into collision with the Swedish law. So, after TV 1 and TV 2, both state managed, came TV3 and very soon the genie was out of the bottle. Swedes today have access to some 30 different TV stations (as well as a large number of radio stations), most financed by advertising. Because of language and force of habit, TV 1 and TV 2 have a strong hold on the viewers.

That, however, is not the end of the story. Far from it...

To describe the development of radio and TV in the US would require a book of its own. Neither is it necessary in this context. Let's content ourselves with saying that the first radio report on a presidential election was transmitted from a garage in Philadelphia. The first political debate in Sweden came four years later (when private radio was still allowed). It featured Per Albin Hansson, Admiral Arvid Lindman, and two leading politicians, CG Ekman and Ivan Bratt (best known as the man behind the rationing of alcoholic beverages, which was sometimes called the Bratt System).

While the development of electronic media dragged out in Sweden, in the US it exploded. No doubt because advertising and mass audiences made it possible to make loads of money, radio and TV stations were established everywhere, even in the most unlikely places. The US soon got the three big networks, NBC, CBS and ABC, covering the continent and being more and more important in public affairs. In a few years it became almost impossible - to make only the most important point - to win an election without having enough money to spend on TV advertising. Indeed, the big winners in any election became the networks.

The networks and the public. The dominance of the three big ones came to an end in the late 70's and early 80's when cable TV and satellite transmissions made it possible for local stations (so called super stations) to cover wider areas and offer a plethora of new programming. Most important of the newcomers was without doubt Ted Turner's CNN (Cable News Network), which in 1980 started to transmit news 24 hours a day, seven days a week. It took a long time for CNN to make much of an impact, but after the Gulf War of 1991, all-news TV took off. In a few years we got BBC World, exclusively devoted to news; media magnate Rupert Murdoch launched Sky News and Fox News (which very quickly became number one in terms of viewership), and both CNBC and MSNBC got into the competition. All in all, long before Sweden even had o n e commercial station, the ordinary American, rich or poor, had the chance to be better informed of world and domestic events than the citizen of any other country and this by simply watching TV. For somebody who just couldn't bear to watch commercials (or at least not too many of them) there was PBS (Public Broadcasting System), available everywhere and financed mainly by voluntary donations. It should be said that the quality of PBS programs is much higher than what you will find on Swedish or other European state channels, except the BBC; a function, of course, of a large and growing population and the enormous size and wealth of the American market place.

But once again, this is not all…

On any Sunday morning for many, many years, the American networks have given the viewer a chance to watch public affairs programs of the highest quality. There is NBC's Meet the Press, CBS's Face the Nation, ABC's This Week and any number of competitors, nation wide as well as local. Invited guests, mainly politicians, but also economists, authors, business men, and journalists are interviewed by competent, indeed brilliantly well prepared panelists (including quite often correspondents from the New York Times, the Washington Post, Time, Newsweek and others). All kinds of opinions are given their chance; fakes are exposed, bluffs called and news made. Indeed Sunday on American TV is a day of free public education unequaled anywhere.

It is fair to say that pressure from media, not the least of which includes TV, has made American politics very transparent. The debate is out in the open and nobody in authority can afford to stay out of the klieg lights. The President himself is somewhat of an exception. Presidents appear but seldom except for press conferences, although everybody else is more or less forced to explain himself to the interviewers, the cameras, and the public. Americans, as opposed to Europeans, get a chance to know their leaders. It can always be said that this favors the slick and the telegenic. This is perhaps true but honesty shines through, too, and all in all, there is no better system.

It could and should be added that:

1. Because of greater resources, the American networks are superior also in the making of documentaries from religion to the movie industry and other feature programs.

2. Just about the same holds for the Internet, which speaks English with a strongly American accent and will continue to do so.

3. The argument that TV and radio also offer an enormous, indeed overwhelming amount of pure trash just doesn't hold water. Trash there is, by the buckets, but the fact is, after all, that the viewer/consumer decides what to watch. If he/she wants trash, so be it. Force-feeding simply doesn't work; witness the East Bloc. The important thing, therefore, is that quality programming, mainly in the public service sector, is AVAILABLE. And it is.

Well, in the US.

In Sweden the three leading channels have little money and not a lot of enthusiasm left for news or public service programs. There is a horrible sameness in the reporting done by the state channels. TV 1 and TV 2 are both financed by a license fee that is in reality a tax on owning a TV set. Both avoid controversy and in reality always favor the sitting government. TV 4 shadows its two main rivals and offers nothing original. All three manage to offer about one public service program per week and only "in season."

The Sunday mornings I used to love so much when living in the US, are simply not available here.

Taxes in the USA and Sweden as percent of GDP in 1991:
US 29.8 %; Sweden 53.2 %

Buying power per capita in US dollars:
US $22,204; Sweden $16,792

Average amount of savings per family:
US $4,201; Sweden $10,943

(Source: "Where We Stand" by Michael Wolff and the World Bank Research Team.)

5

Staying out of wars—from guilt, to self-congratulation.

Anti-Americanism had hardly existed in Sweden until after the Second World War.

As long as the great conflagration lasted, almost all Swedes followed the troop movements on the European continent with interest and often passion. In the beginning there also was fear. Hitler might win. We might have to fight and die or be enslaved.

Would we be able to defend ourselves? Would the British hold? Would Stalin stop the onslaught?

Would the Americans come to save us?

We all listened to reports about the invasion in Normandy, applauded the brave grunts, and idolized generals like Eisenhower and his British counterpart, Bernard Law Montgomery (with his snappy beret). Each and every little local newspaper printed maps of battles, and in the evening we all sat glued to the old radio sets when famed commentator Bo Enander, greatly admired for his undisguised contempt for the Nazis, explained the thrusts and counter thrusts, analyzed the attacker's strategy, and underlined the necessity that all of Europe must be free so that the lights could go on again (as Vera Lynn sang).

We saw pictures of the GI's and their tanks and jeeps (oh, how badly we little boys wanted to drive jeeps!), and guns and helmets and flak vests, and we loved and admired them. There were Nazis, too, in the country, but hardly among us common folks. We all wanted the Americans to win, although quite a big minority of Communists saw comrade Stalin as a liberator, too.

Sometimes American or British flyers parachuted from damaged planes or managed crash landings on our soil. People cried with happiness if and when they were found safe and sound; we saw them all as heroes, who had probably killed thousands of Germans (as indeed sometimes they had). Germans, on the other hand, were hardly considered human. In Sweden, they were so despised, that even decades after the war German tourists got a very chilly reception in Sweden. They were better treated in Denmark and Norway, in spite of the fact that both countries had been occupied.

In those days, if somebody had said something negative about America, he would have been challenged to any number of fistfights.

And then it all changed.

The turnaround began, of course, with politicians, intellectuals, and other makers of opinion: what is generally known as the elite. Exactly what happened and why it happened will never be known, but with hindsight a few of the reasons become clear.

First, there was a sense of guilt.

When the war broke out, Sweden declared herself neutral, which was, in retrospect, perfectly sensible. We would, in other words, not go to war unless the country was attacked, presumably by the Germans. Our defenses were not strong: hardly any tanks, no artillery to speak of, and no air force worthy of the name. If Hitler had wanted, he could have taken Sweden as easily as he took Norway and Denmark; the Danes hardly tried to defend themselves at all and the Norwegians were quickly subdued. Both countries were occupied and suffered considerably until Germany's capitulation on May 8, 1945.

For Sweden, however, Hitler and his strategists had different and more important plans. In my opinion, the country was to become an extension of Germany's war industry. The government took care—Swedes are not fools—to trade with the UK as well and to some small extent with the US and other allied countries, but only Germany really counted.

Briefly, it happened like this:

When the war broke out, Prime Minister Per Albin Hansson went on radio (a state monopoly at the time through well into the 80's, see Chapter 4). He spoke, as always, in a heavy voice, an honest workman bringing bad news:

"The horrible thing that we hoped the world would be spared has now happened. A new great war has started. We must accept this horrible fact and there is little to gain from trying to express the sorrow and terror we feel while thinking of the anguish and pain it might bring to an already lacerated and pained humanity…"

Only a few days earlier, on August 27, the Prime Minister had given another important speech, in which he claimed that our preparedness is good. This was reasonably true as far as supplies in general were concerned. Sweden was much better off than on the eve of the First World War when food stocks were very low. There was no risk of starvation. MILITARY defense on the other hand, was, as already noted, in very bad shape. Sweden might have been able to put up some kind of organized resistance for a couple of weeks, hardly more.

A few days after the sudden German attack on Poland, Per Albin and his aides traveled to Copenhagen, Denmark, for a meeting with the prime and foreign ministers of the Nordic countries. The meeting was conducted in an atmosphere of insecurity and crisis, which is quite understandable as nobody really had anything but very vague ideas about what was to follow.

The Prime Minister left an official party a bit early and instead took Gunnar Hägglöf (a star diplomat for many decades) to the outdoor café of the famed Hotel d'Angleterre, where they had a couple of beers. The Father of the Country (as he was known for some time) was in a talkative mood and quite happy to have left everyday stress and problems behind in Stockholm.

"Here in Copenhagen, when we have been discussing all sorts of things, I have been able to close my eyes and think," he said.

He drained his first Carlsberg and confessed that he had never believed that the nations that had suffered so grievously in the First World War would ever be sucked into another catastrophe.

"But Hitler and Mussolini have preached the Gospel of War for a long time," Hägglöf insisted. He and several of his colleagues had long been warning the government that war was inevitable.

The dialogue that followed is revealing and in my opinion truly frightening.

"But this is what scares me the most," Per Albin said. "Emperors, czars, and a European upper class brought on the First World War but both Hitler and Mussolini stem from the working class. How can they want to go to war? A war that will cost the working classes so much suffering...."

Recalling the conversation, Hägglöf writes that Per Albin spoke with passion, a passion he very seldom showed as openly as that evening.

"It is really hell," the prime minister said, "that all my comrades and I have achieved now will be destroyed. We have wished for social equality, security for sick and old people and a lot of other things. For the Now we will have to concentrate everything on military enterprises, artillery, battle ships and airplanes. Isn't it hell?"

If Hägglöf's recollection is correct (which I have every reason to believe) the conversation over the beer glasses at d´Angleterre was one of those rare events when fundamental truths are suddenly laid bare. Three points are particularly important:

1) Per Albin had never given much thought to foreign policy or problems connected with national security. The First World War had spared Sweden. The Russian Revolution had not spilled over and the Social Democrats had won power at the ballot box. He now thought that it would be possible to arrange the world in a peaceful and proper way, just as he intended to make Sweden a nice and clean and orderly place for everybody. That irrational feelings play a great role in the relations between states as well as human beings he refused to understand; that leaders can be insane; that evil exists; that chance is a leading player and that accidents happen; notions of that kind, he resolutely ignored. This seems perhaps even stranger when one knows that Per Albin actually had parallel relationships running with two women over a long period of time and fought many passionately personal battles on the political arena. He was certainly not naive in the meaning one normally assigns to the word. But he was blindly focused on the construction of *Folkhemmet Sverige* (the "people's home Sweden"), the perfect welfare state, by necessity an isolationist, and in the context of the Great War, instinctively neutral. Not for the first time and absolutely not for the last, the Swedes saw the outside world as a disorderly and dangerous place. They managed to find only one solution:

They turned their backs and became inward looking. Only very few hotheads wanted to join the Allied cause; the country's greatest publicist of the time, Torgny Segerstedt, was widely admired for his attacks on Hitler, but the realists running the country found him to be just a pain in the ass.

2) What Per Albin said about Hitler and Mussolini belonging to the

working class and therefore should have automatically known better than to make war, is disturbing, at least to me. To ascribe to the class to which one belongs, or in the case of Per Albin, the purer and nobler class one has become a powerful representative of, is to misunderstand what democracy is all about. That is to say that INDIVIDUALS are what counts, regardless of race, gender, birth, or indeed, class. To romanticize the working class was indeed already a habit among left wing politicians, a habit that started to slowly wane only towards the end of the century, when the working class had become rather middle and therefore had become wage earners in political parlance.

3) Most important is the paragraph that starts with isn't it hell. With this comment, "isn't it hell," Per Albin complains about social equality, health care. In brief, the welfare state would be threatened because of the dictators being so bloody minded?

Once more this strange tunnel vision, this subconscious confession in a relaxed moment, that democracy itself, in solidarity with the people attacked and violated, were secondary questions. Morality was but a word, and after all, those who fought turned out to be foreigners. Only Social-Sverige, the perfect welfare state really counted.

Am I pressing my interpretation of the background to the conversation too far? I don't think so. And in any case the intention is to emphasize, as strongly as possible, how the welfare project had already become more important than everything else. The outside world had become a disturbance or, in the worst case, a threat.

At another occasion Per Albin actually spoke of the Swedes as peace-egotists. No doubt he knew what of he was speaking. Also, a very important and undeniable fact shows how the government viewed the world:

In 1936, with war rapidly approaching, the Social Democratic leadership, which Per Albin dominated, decided on a ten-year plan for the defense of Sweden. It called for a very slow upgrading of the military forces just as if there was no reason in the world to worry about war. Consequently, when war broke out after three years of modernizing, the Swedish Army was in lamentable shape. An infantry regiment (Hägglöf wrote) had to rely on two 8-millimeter machine guns for its air defense and two 37-millimeter canons to fight off tanks. In other words, the equipment was about as efficient as the lances wielded by the Polish cavalry; a German attack would have meant massacre of badly trained conscripts, and in most cases, their rather incompetent officers. Especially the weakness of the air defense is incomprehensible, as a Swedish company, Bofors, had developed (partially with German aid) a truly remarkable 40-milli-meter canon. It would later be sold all around the world, including in the US, and it indeed became the best selling artillery piece EVER. Sweden, though, did not yet consider it worth defense money.

Per Albin, of course, knew for a long time that Germany rearmed; he just shied away from understanding what it meant. Since the time of the First World War he was clearly conscious of the importance of Swedish iron ore for the Kaiser's war machine, and now the Germans once more bought all the ore the Swedes could produce. The truth is that all reasonably well informed people in Europe knew full well that Germany could not make war— at least not over an extended period of time— without access to iron ore from Sweden.

Had the Swedes refused to sell, the country would no doubt have been attacked. But the extraction of iron ore is easily sabotaged and the miners in northern Sweden, a great many of whom were communists, would have given the occupation troops serious problems. So would allied bombing raids and perhaps commando operations. The vital ball bearing plants in Gothenburg could have been taken out or at least badly damaged, and all in all, it is quite possible that a NOT neutral Sweden would have shortened the war by as much as two years, as the eminent American historian William Shirer has claimed.

Many Swedes knew all this and not a few felt badly about it. Others fought and died for freedom and democracy. We, the Swedes, profited. It felt like we had blood on our hands, that we were guilty of treason against democracy.

But this changed.

Sweden's attitude towards the US and the world, as it developed after the war, can only be understood as a result of domestic, political considerations. In brief, the picture looks like this:

We were saved.

Unlike most others we were not hurt and did not bleed. The sense of shame and non-belonging soon started to transform into less and less subtle self-congratulation. We could produce, others could not; in that respect we were, hmm... better. We could sell all we produced; others had no choice but to buy. We prospered; for all others, except the US, prosperity was long in coming - and the US was very far away from Europe. In spite of the fact that so many, many Swedes had gone to the US during the preceding one hundred years, knowledge of the great country in the west was quite limited. Before the war, Swedes who traveled, did so in Europe as it was simply too expensive and too time consuming to go to the States. As a matter of fact, no Swedish leader set foot in the New World until well after WWII.

Others, however, most certainly did. In 1952, when Tage Erlander became the first prime minister to visit over there, a trickle of business people and students had gone to see the country that was suddenly on top of the world. Young and old discovered the magic of the automobile and the drive-in movie, of fast food, orange juice, and cowboy boots. Both the travelers and those who stayed at home tasted their first Coca-Cola, the fantastic drink that became the very symbol of American cultural expansion. American universities, spearheaded by Harvard, Yale, and Colombia, and a little bit later UCLA and Berkley, became favored destinations for everybody with sufficient resources. And for those who had no resources the student ex-change programs soon opened up. Thousands upon thousands of American families (not necessarily affluent, but always generous) opened their homes to Swedes, Dutch, Danes, and all the others to spend a year to study at an American high school or college. Some American youngsters made the opposite trek to Europe, but in general, education became a one-way street. To have an American education became a sign of quality. You had seen the future and realized how big it was; you had learned to speak the more and more dominant language; you were part of the modern world. A *sammanträde* (Swedish for meeting) during the 1950's became known as a meeting, and words like markcting, sales promotion, and, of course PR, became and still are Swedish as well as English words.

Behind the words there were processes and methods, ways of doing things. In Sweden the first companies to hire PR men (in the beginning only men needed apply!) were the importers of American movies, usually affiliated with Hollywood. When I came to Stockholm in 1955, the young, well-dressed and well-groomed men who made their living plugging this or that movie were already ubiquitous. So were the two (or five) martini lunches they chalked up to their expense account. Stars like James Dean, Marlon Brando, and of course, Ava Gardner, Grace Kelly, and the rat pack (led by Sinatra) became great idols. The same could be said for authors like Hemingway and Norman Mailer. No self-respecting magazine or tabloid could do without a gossip column from Hollywood. (I wrote many myself during my first post in New York 1963-75.)

From the movie companies the importance of good public relations spread to real industry. In Sweden before, during, and immediately after the war, the press did not cover business and industry very well. If a journalist wanted to check something out he usually called the switchboard and asked for the CEO. After the request had been turned down, as it regularly was, he simply asked who would be willing to talk to him, after which he was directed to an obscure engineer or salesman who almost always had very, very little to say. The contrast to today's armies of information officers is indeed striking; so is the availability of CEO's.

In the late 50's, Volvo, having just started an intensivedrive to sell cars in the US, decided that the time had come to get PR. Famed CEO Gunnar Engelau made an attempt to hire the country's most popular radio reporter/ sportscaster/ entertainer, Lennart Hyland. The attempt failed in spite of the fact that Hyland was offered a salary of $20,000 a year, a truly fantastic sum in those days. Instead, Captain Hans Blenner, who had organized Queen Elizabeth's highly successful state visit to Stockholm in 1955, was approached. Blenner traveled to Gothenburg where he met Engelau.

"We have to have PR," the big man said, according to anecdote.

"What do you want me to do?" asked Blenner.

"That you will (expletive deleted) have to find out for yourself," said Engelau.

Blenner took the job. When he quit a couple of decades later, he had become one of the most important councilors to Engelau, and then to the latter's successor (and son-in-law), Pehr G. Gyllenhammar. The information department counted many hundred employees the world around.

All serious Swedish companies developed along similar lines, always seeking guidance first and foremost from the US.

The few Swedes who did not jump over to the US but preferred to travel in Europe in the years immediately after 1945 understood that poverty and destruction there—people were living in huts and holes in once- shining cities like Hamburg as well as Berlin and Dresden! —was a confirmation of the wisdom of staying out of the war. The war obviously had been evil. If we had joined, the argument went, we would have had to suffer, too, and to what end? Now we could help in rebuilding (albeit for money!) and offer good advice on how create a peaceful, civilized, and prosperous society. If we could do it, they ought to be able to do it, too, at least if they realized how wrong headed they had been.

I do not mean that the travelers phrased their thoughts the way I have done, but subconsciously most felt that we, the Swedes, had been smarter. We had not been humiliated and we didn't have to beg. So, we must have been doing something right…

Right?

In the first Olympic games after the war, held in London in 1948, well-fed and well-trained Swedes took a lot of medals in track and field, football, and other disciplines. This also—perhaps not surprisingly—was taken as an indication of the superior quality of the Swedish model.

Even if that expression itself was not yet in use.

It should be added that Swedes in general (but not the mainly Stockholm based elite) took to things American, everything from chewing gum and Coke to movies and business practices, with great enthusiasm. In the 1960's we started to say that Sweden was the most Americanized country in the world.

Number two was the United States.

The Gross Domestic Product (GDP) of the USA in 2006 was $13,244,550,000. On the list, compiled by the International Monetary Fund (IMF) the US ranks #2, after the European Union.

Sweden's GDP the same year was $385,292,000, which makes the country #19 on the list.

6

World power

In the closing days of the Great War, Roosevelt met Churchill and Stalin in an old czarist resort near the Crimean city of Yalta.

The American President was sick and weak, in fact dying. He and Churchill effectively recognized Soviet hegemony in Eastern Europe and thus helped set the stage for what later became known as the Cold War.

In the view of many conservatives, the dying Roosevelt did nothing less at Yalta than sell out Eastern Europe to Soviet control for the next 50 years. In the view of liberals, including major historians, Roosevelt ceded Poland and parts of Eastern Europe to Stalin because the Red Army controlled the territory anyway. He had no choice and whatever was said at Yalta would have changed no realities on the ground. The agreement also called for free elections in Poland, a call that Stalin ignored and had always planned to ignore.

So, there was great suspicion dividing the allies, but, perhaps more important, they still WERE allies.

George W. Bush and conservatives like Pat Buchanan would later put Yalta on par with the Munich Pact of 1938 and the Molotov-Ribbentrop Pact of 1939. Most others would see this as a wild exaggeration. The important thing in the context of this book was that an American president now had to deal as much with arranging and rearranging the world as with governing his own country. It had in fact been that way from at least the time of Abraham Lincoln, but after the First and particularly the Second World War the pronouncement of a US president, whether one liked or not, had repercussions everywhere. The man in the White House was the most powerful man in the world, a fact made even more obvious by better communications. Gradually more and more people all around the globe started to follow the goings on in Washington—not yet an imperial capital, but on its way—with almost the same interest they followed politics in their own countries. The old power centers, London, Paris, and Berlin, seemed more and more like burnt out stars or maybe monuments over a glorious past.

The trend, as we know, would continue.

To say that it didn't create resentment would be lying. Politicians in France, a country that once ruled about 10 percent of the world, spoke darkly of Americans as at once ignorant and arrogant. The Brits were a bit more hospitable, but even they and most others were more than a little jealous. A strange schizophrenia developed. A politician could score points in his or her home country by standing up to the Yanks, but it could just as well be helpful to have visited the White House, and it soon became de rigueur (!) to have talked with the great man fifteen minutes or so longer than scheduled. Afterwards, one could claim that the President had really been SO interested in what the representative of country A, B or C had had to say…

Politicians are by nature ambitious and eager to make decisions in matters big and small, to shape their countries and the world. This goes for Swedish politicians just as well as all others. The problem, of course, is that Sweden is very small and has no weight to throw around. So, one of the most important reasons the two countries started to drift apart, was that the little one had very little reason to think in world terms, whereas the superpower was forced to do so. The US, whether its leaders liked it or not became *responsible*.

Swedish leaders might feel equally responsible and better qualified, but unluckily nobody cared. Partly as a result of this the country became more and more inward looking with every passing year while the US, sometimes grudgingly, went on to become involved in countless conflicts and crises, often in faraway places of which the average American new little or nothing. Isolationism was no longer an option for the leaders of the country and its intellectual, commercial, and scientific elite.

Needless to say, the corresponding elites in Sweden were involved, too. The difference was, once again, that whatever Americans said was always and automatically important. What Swedes said or thought mattered little - a fact much disliked around Stockholm.

With communications improving rapidly and media year after year painting a clearer picture of the world, it was only natural that, say, a Swedish Prime Minister put himself in an American President's shoes.

Was Roosevelt right when he left Eastern Europe to Stalin? Was Truman wrong when he proclaimed his Doctrine of 1947 and stopped the Russians from gobbling up Greece?

You could hear both opinions in Sweden, of course. What is important to know is that the men and women (still very few of them) that took part in the debate were quite unable to influence anything happening on the ground. This is probably the main reason why momentous events out there in the world became a backdrop for fights that were really almost always about domestic matters in Sweden. Slowly, the outside world became more and more unreal. The fact that we became more and more dependent on it didn't seem to register. What mattered was Sweden. We could lecture and condemn, and did, but the really important thing was to keep Sweden a place where we could live in peace and prosperity, preferably without being disturbed.

We couldn't stop the world and get off, but we could turn our backs to it and look at each other. That, we did.

Well, of course, we also wanted as much recognition as possible. When Dag Hammarskjöld was elected Secretary General of the United Nations in 1953, it was widely taken as convincing proof that the states of the world, powers both great and small, in fact realized that Sweden was a special case, small in population and power, but abundantly in possession of objective wisdom. That Hammarskjöld himself held a quite unrealistic opinion of the powers of his office has really never been realized in his home country.

The United States inspired and strongly supported the unification of Europe. It is fair to say that left to the Europeans it would not have happened, or it might have happened much later and in a much different way.

In reality Sweden opposed it, refused to side with the democracies, and particularly during the many years of Olof Palme's premiership actually sought to gain influence in the world by actively supporting a third way between East and West. If you want to press the argument to the very limit, you could say that the Swedes actually sought to sabotage the world structure the US attempted to build.

The story really begins with the Bomb.

On August 6th 1945, the first, crude nuclear bomb used in war was detonated over the Japanese city of Hiroshima. Harry Truman, the little Vice President, who had not been in the know about the Manhattan

Project, which created the ultimate weapon, didn't hesitate to give the go ahead for the use of it. If he had not, the US would have had to invade one or several of Japan's main islands suffering tens of thousands of casualties, a most disagreeable prospect.

So, Truman really didn't have a choice. Neither he, nor anybody else in authority believed that the atomic monopoly would last very long. The genie was out of the bottle and could not be put back in, neither by international agreements, nor by other means. It seemed quite certain that the Soviets would try to come up with an answer, which is, of course, precisely what happened, leading to an armament race that only ended with the demise of the Soviet Union in 1991 (and in many respects not even then). Almost nobody thought that the bomb would in fact protect the world from another catastrophic war.

In Sweden a strong anti- bomb opinion soon developed, but more importantly, the government for quite some time discussed whether we ought to have the bomb, too. After all, Sweden at the time had the world's third or fourth largest air force and sufficient technological capacity. Or at least this is how the thinking was. Olof Palme almost certainly was one of the leading friends of the bomb; so were many of the country's generals. American leaders like John F. Kennedy were conscious of Sweden's efforts and very much against them. American diplomats in Stockholm were instructed to encourage Sweden to keep a solid defense (which was done) but to stay away from the Bomb, which would destabilize the situation in Northern Europe without corresponding gains.

The fact that peace was not to break out after the worst war in history soon became apparent. Eastern Europe remained occupied and it soon became evident that the US and the Soviet Union would become, if not enemies, at least ideological competitors.

Who were the Russians? What did they want?

The best answer came in perhaps the most important diplomatic communication in history. The sender was a senior US diplomat in Moscow, George Kennan, who (begging forgiveness for overloading the telegraph!) on February 22, 1946, sent the State Department The Long Telegram in which he stated the USSR under Stalin was impervious to the logic of reason but highly sensitive to the logic of force. The Communists, Kennan wrote, must be contained, stopped in their tracks and not allowed to subjugate other states and peoples. You could deal successfully with them only from a position of strength.

Kennan rewrote his telegram into an article in the magazine Foreign

Affairs. For diplomatic reasons he was, after all, accredited in Moscow, and accordingly he signed the piece X. It immediately became required reading in Washington; containment became the fundament of the US and its allies' policy towards the Soviets for more than fifty years, indeed until the Soviet Union was no more.

Things were moving fast. On Stalin's orders the Russians supported the communist guerrilla in Greece and made menacing demands on Turkey. The UK was still suffering economically from the war efforts and let it be known that it could not be relied on for help. Its days as a great power were over. Only the US had the capacity to stop the onslaught and contain the Russians behind their own borders.

This Truman decided to do. He managed to get Congress to support aid to the two countries and on the 12th of March 1947, proclaimed the Truman Doctrine, which quite clearly stated that:

"I believe it must be the policy of the United States to support free peoples who are resisting subjugation by armed minorities or by outside pressures."

According to anecdote, at about the same time as the Truman Doctrine was prepared, Will Clayton, a Texas businessman turned Under Secretary for Economic Affairs, sauntered into his office at the State Department after a rather liquid lunch and let it be known that we shall have to do something about Europe. Clayton had earlier visited Western Europe and reported first hand about strikes, unemployment, and food shortages—in other words, a quickly worsening crisis. Millions of people are slowly starving, he wrote and shared his on-the-scene impressions with remarkable men like Dean Acheson, Charles Chip Bohlen, Kennan and, of course, the Secretary of State, George Marshall. All agreed that, "we shall have to do something."

Naturally, it fell on Marshall to deliver the speech that launched the plan, officially named The European Recovery Act but soon known as the Marshall Plan. The Secretary of State, speaking on the 5th of June 1947 at Harvard University, dramatically claimed that the patient is sinking, while the doctors are deliberating. The plan, he said, is directed not against any country or doctrine but against hunger, poverty, desperation and chaos.

This was not quite true. The US wanted Europe to prosper and become a market for American products, but it most certainly also wanted the Europeans to be strong enough to keep the Soviets out or at least to stop them long enough for help from the US to arrive.

The mistake of withdrawing and losing influence, as one had done after the First World War, would NOT be repeated. The US, with tens of thousands of soldiers on the Continent, in fact became a European power, in reality by far the leading one. With the passing of time, the Europeans liked this fact less and less, but it remained, and remains, a fact.

In a stroke of genius the Europeans were asked to design the recovery plan themselves. The Soviet Union was invited to join, but refused, together with its Eastern European satellites. Finland also said no, hard pressed by Stalin, who was convinced, no doubt correctly, that close collaboration with the West would draw his countries into the orbit of the US.

The plan was a fantastic success. When the US stopped providing money in 1951 (when the Korean War broke out), it had handed over 13.3 billion dollars, the equivalent of about 100 billion in 2005. Sweden got 347 million, more than several countries that had suffered considerably more. The money was mostly used to buy American foodstuff. It helped Europe to achieve record economic growth between the years 1948 and 1952. That the free trade between countries created by the plan and the infusion of money did more than almost anything else to save the continent from Communism, there can be no doubt.

The political situation steadily deteriorated mainly because Stalin wanted to consolidate his hold over Eastern Europe as swiftly as possible. A coup in February 1948 gave Czechoslovakia a communist government; on Stalin's orders arrests and executions went on all over Eastern Europe (as well as, of course, inside the Soviet Union itself). On the 23rd of June the same year the Berlin blockade was launched in an attempt to force the allied forces out from the enclave that was to become the German Democratic Republic (DDR) in October of 1949.

The blockade was countered by the great airlift that supplied the city with all necessities for almost a year; all in all 277,728 sorties were flown. Dozens of aircrafts were circling the airports waiting to land at all times of the day as well as night. By the time the Soviets relented in May 1949, it was all too clear that peace and brotherhood would not break out any day soon.

In 1946, Winston Churchill had warned of the coming confrontation and the Iron Curtain. The communist parties in France and Italy were large and could very well gain power. As for military power, the Soviet Union was bled dry and in terrible shape—it had lost some 20 million lives but so had Western Europe.

The logical solution was a military alliance between Europe and the US. It was named the North Atlantic Treaty Organization (NATO) and soon enough included a rearmed Western Germany. NATO, the saying went, was created to keep the Americans in, the Soviets out, and the Germans down. Sweden, as we will see in the next chapter worked actively against it, only to join in a secret and sneaky way not officially revealed to the Swedish public before 1994. Indeed, it became almost an article of faith for Swedish politicians to tell their voters that never, ever would neutral Sweden join an organization so clearly designed to use military force to defend Europe (and in reality that included Sweden).

NATO became the military arm of western defense. The European Economic Community, later the European Community and nowadays the European Union, took upon itself two giant tasks, one openly stated, the other more implied. It was to use free trade, open borders and interstate cooperation to increase the prosperity of states and ordinary European citizens. By doing this it was to show the world that democracy and free markets easily beat state planning and command economies—in other words, Socialism and Communism.

It should be noted that the EU might well have been something quite different. In the US, a much discussed plan authored by Secretary of Commerce Hans Morgenthau wanted to force Germany to become an agricultural country, bereft of any industrial capacity and therefore unable to make war. Luckily the proposal didn't fly. At the same time the great Jean Monnet proposed that France take over Germany's steel industry so that it would never be able to rearm (and attack France). The versatile Monnet soon changed his mind and instead proposed a cartel between the coal and steel companies in France, Germany, and the Benelux countries. The leaders bought the plan. Thus, ironically, the greatest free trade area in the world began as a cartel.

Sweden wanted no part of… just about anything.

In his memoirs, Prime Minister Tage Erlander makes clear that the coup in Prague as well as the Berlin blockade worried him very much, just as the Korean War did later (and in 1961 the crisis between the Soviet Union and Finland). "There wasn't much we (Sweden) could do," Erlander stated gloomily.

But one thing we could do. We could refuse to join either of the blocs.

Not only that. Sweden made it a policy to try to make all of Scandinavia (Denmark, Norway, and Sweden) a neutral bloc. Sweden proposed a

Scandinavian defense alliance, and during 1948-49 negotiations involved politicians, diplomats and military men. The Swedish intention was to create a kind of third force between NATO and the Soviets. Sweden had, we thought, Erlander later wrote, no serious differences of opinion, with either of the blocs.

This was not at all true. For one thing, there was no possibility—none at all—that the US, alone, together with Great Britain, or in any other way would invade Sweden, or indeed any of the other Nordic countries. Only the Soviet Union was close enough and had sufficient military resources to do that. It was not known at the time that Stalin actually dreamed of advancing when the US was held in check by China in Korea as far west as Spain, but the suspicion that the Communists harbored expansionar intentions was widely spread. Erlander, as mentioned, was clearly worried, even if his Foreign Minister, Östen Undén, who had a visceral aversion to the US and everything American saw no evil and heard no evil.

The negotiations about the Scandinavian Defense Alliance were, in a sense, an attempt to sabotage NATO. As it were the talks went nowhere. Norway and Denmark, who had both been occupied, to no one's surprise, chose NATO. So, to a very large extent did Sweden. But, of course, not in the open. A long period of deceit commenced.

In 1974, Erlander wrote about hints from, among others, leading militaries that Sweden ought to make preparations for receiving help from the West in case of war. He tells us he saw these hints with grave concern. Maybe some observers abroad would see the hints as confirmation that such cooperation was already in progress.

In fact, Erlander (but probably not Undén) knew very well that exactly the cooperation he denied was well under way. He chose to lie even decades after the fact. The Swedish Air Force kept in close touch with the US headquarters in Wiesbaden, Germany. Sweden was allowed to buy military equipment just like it had been a full fledged NATO partner indeed; a little further down the road, our fighter-bombers would not have been able to fly without quite a few American components (among them a jet engine built on license). Already in the 1950's, at some Swedish air bases the runways were lengthened so that they could receive American bombers that, if and when worst came to worst, would bomb the Soviets. Concrete plans foresaw that Sweden's defense staff would operate out of bases in the UK and so on.

Everything was ready, but very, very few people knew it and none has spoken. It wasn't until decades later that Swedes in general were to know, among other things, that a certain William Colby, later to become director of the CIA and America's foremost spymaster, worked in Sweden in the 1950's to build a clandestine, voluntary force of Swedes that should fight an occupation force. A later well-known insurance executive, Alvar Lindencrona headed parallel, Swedish efforts.

How all this would have worked in the tug of war is, of course, an entirely different matter.

Discussing the (surreptitiously) not so neutral neutrality, Erlander wrote:

"How does the workingman feel? The farmer? If I'm not mistaken, he is worried that we will be dragged into something that is not our business, but that can cost our lives... let us be honest, they (the Swedish people) want peace at almost any price."

Erlander was very fearful that the Russians would decide to strike in 1951 before the West was rearmed and ready. Because of Simon Sebag Montefiori's invaluable book about the Soviet leader we now know that the fear was quite warranted. Stalin could have stopped the UN from backing the US intervention in Korea, but he chose *not* to do it. In fact he wanted the war very much; China and America making each other weaker was a dream come true for the men in the Kremlin.

Tage Erlander, of course, didn't know Stalin's thinking. He didn't like communists, but he was, after all a man of the left, surrounded by people who simply refused to believe even when confronted with overwhelming evidence that Stalin was a brutal murderer who wanted as much power as possible and abided by agreements only when it suited him.

Did Erlander really believe that the Russians would have respected Sweden's neutrality if there had been a war in Europe? Would the men in the Kremlin let the construction of the Folkhemmet go on unabated? Why would Sweden be treated better than other nations?

The Prime Minister offers no clues to his thinking. But there is no other answer than that we would have been enslaved, just like the others.

The Americans solved the Swedish problem in a rather sophisticated way. The Truman and Eisenhower administrations simply decided that a militarily reasonably strong Sweden was in the best interest of the US and that if Sweden was attacked, the US would come to its assistance. According to Anders Thunborg, who was for a while Palme's defense minister, nothing was said officially, but when he visited the Pentagon, it was made absolutely clear that Sweden was really inside the Western

Alliance, it just didn't quite know about it.

We read the map, the Americans told Thunborg. Meaning: Sweden lies between Russia and NATO member Norway. It would be almost impossible to defend Norway without also defending Sweden. So a unilateral and secret security guaranty was decided upon.

Most Swedes still don't know about this. The false and hypocritical neutrality became more than a policy, almost a religion, used by the Social Democratic party for its own purposes.

When Tage Erlander decided to accept an invitation to the US, the Soviet ambassador in Stockholm complained that the Swedish Prime Minister ought to visit Moscow before Washington because it was closer. Erlander, who was a humoristic man, replied that if the Russians could find eight of his cousins in their country—he had that many in the US—he would perhaps reconsider. What the Russian said is not known, but on April 3rd 1952, Erlander took off from Bromma airport to visit his cousins and President Truman. His main concern was his bad English (which was truly horrible).

President Truman, who had already decided not to run for reelection, invited Erlander for lunch. Nothing of importance was discussed, maybe mainly because all serious discussions took place at the military level and in conversations between Marcus Wallenberg and various American power brokers. To touch the problems at the highest political level would only have been counterproductive.

On the 13th of June, not very long after Erlander's return to Sweden, a Soviet jet fighter shot down the Swedish DC-3 Hugin over the Baltic. Three days later the Soviets downed an amphibious Catalina aircraft looking for the DC-3.

Nobody knew, outside the innermost circles in Stockholm and Washington, that the Hugin was a spy plane (although many suspected it). It was crammed with sophisticated electronics provided the Swedish Air Force from the US. It was understood that the Swedes would share their observations with the Pentagon. The deal was so secret that not even the Swedish Foreign Minister, Östen Undén, who detested the US, was in the know. Indeed, all cabinet members except Erlander's friends Torsten Nilsson and Sven Andersson were kept out of the loop.

Unluckily the same didn't hold true for Air Force Colonel Stig Wennerström, who took up a position as military attaché in Washington just before Erlander's visit. Wennerström was a spy for the Soviets for many years. He had access to just about everything there was to know about Sweden's defense forces and defense plans. So, to sum it up: the decision makers both in Washington and the Kremlin were much, much better informed than the Swedish public and even the Swedish cabinet. The Russians, quite frankly, considered the Swedish neutrality a stupid hoax. It played well in Swedish domestic politics, but not in Moscow.

Erlander visited the US two more times and met with leading officials. His successor, Olof Palme, was never welcomed.

7

Sweden—the world's conscience

As I wrote in the preceding chapter, Sweden tried to sabotage NATO, only to become its silent and secret partner.

That the secret was known to some insiders in Washington and most likely to the men in the Kremlin mattered little. To Prime Minister Erlander and his most trusted associates, the most important thing was that the Swedish people should not know. So they lied. And beat their own drums. Neutrality and freedom from entangling alliances became a way of making the country, small that it is, much more important in the world. We did not join the crowd, any crowd. Tall and independent, the Swede walked his own way, thought his own thoughts, and felt free to criticize the West as well as the East. Sweden, the country that escaped the war (and made good money from it) became the self-proclaimed referee in world affairs.

The world's conscience, some of us said, disapprovingly. Much more importantly, the overwhelming majority did NOT disapprove. Many felt, like Per Albin Hansson, that those who remained neutral were morally superior to people who fought wars. So by going it alone, Sweden, like France and the US, could lay claim to be an exceptional, outstanding nation.

Sweden's intellectuals, then as now, were overwhelmingly leftists. Most claimed to be strong internationalists but were in many ways rather chauvinistic, quite convinced that anybody who took sides in the great conflict was un-Swedish and irresponsible, indeed almost criminal. A kind of particularly Swedish McCarthyism developed in the form of a mindset that became known as the Third Opinion (*Tredje Ståndpunkten*).

We, the Swedes, it was claimed, were endowed with considerably more common sense than other people. We could build bridges and make adversaries compromise. We were more *lagom* than anybody else (lagom, a Swedish word impossible to translate, roughly means better balanced, less driven by emotions and less prone to excesses than other, non-Swedish human beings).

Swedes, to put it plainly, were the best.

The leaders of the Third Opinion group were authors Karl Vennberg, Artur Lundkvist, Erwin Leiser and Stig Carlsson, all convinced socialists and more or less undistinguishable from the Social Democrats who largely sympathized with them. In his memoirs, Tage Erlander wrote:

"Their worldview was… deeply pessimistic. Their fear that the world would come to an end in a new war was so strong that it approached certainty… they saw the Swedish policy of neutrality as a glimmer of hope. They supported the policy of the government, but were upset over the government's inability to see through the American propaganda… Their opinion that one should not choose between east and west but follow an independent neutral policy, they called the Third Opinion…"

Artur Lundkvist was, together with Vennberg, the most pugnacious in the group, whom very few intellectuals dared oppose during the 1950's. A brilliant exception was NATO-supporter Herbert Tingsten, editor-in-chief for the leading daily, *Dagens Nyheter*. Tingsten stressed that there really is quite a difference between democracy and dictatorship. For his trouble he was labeled reactionary and a lackey of the US, epithets that for five decades would be used against everybody who did not criticize the US in harsher terms (preferably much harsher!) than the Soviet Union.

One of the country's most important authors, Eyvind Johnson, made known that he was on the side of freedom and democracy. For this, he was roundly condemned as primitive and demagogic. Indeed, whoever said an unkind word about the Soviet Union—be it Gulag or dictatorship—was quickly branded a supporter of McCarthyism.

The Third Opinion was not clear-cut communism, but almost. All supporters of the view called themselves socialists and all were in favor of collective solutions to social and political problems (that is for the people, but not for the elite to which they were certain they belonged). In an article in *Morgon-Tidningen*, which spoke for the government, Lundkvist wrote that "..it is not less important to defend oneself against capitalism than against dictatorial communism…irresponsible capitalistic competition… clearly leads to catastrophe. The alternative is to more or less thoroughly follow socialist principles…"

Again, Lundkvist's socialism was not communism, but almost. The headline over the article really told the whole story. It read:

'DEMOCRACY DEMANDS SOCIALISM'

Lundkvist, like Olof Palme later on, became more and more of a revolutionary romantic who soon would praise Fidel, Che Guevara, Ho Chi Minh and a whole lot of other self styled freedom fighters, who liberated nothing, but enslaved a lot.

Tage Erlander thought highly of Lundkvist (an insufferably self-important man) and the other Third Opinioners. As I have already told, in his memoirs the Prime Minister lies by omitting the truth - about Sweden's NATO connection. Instead he quotes a government document that very explicitly states that Sweden sees itself as a moral great power. The balance of power in the world would change dramatically if Sweden chose sides, the document says. Than it goes all out:

"We don't imagine that we have a possibility to… build bridges between the two present big power groupings. On the other hand it can hardly be conceived to believe that seen in an international perspective it might be valuable if we strive to successively develop a type of society that confers both political and economical democracy, a society… which by its structure demonstrates a true political democracy with room for real social justice."

Translated to ordinary prose, the tortured sentences can mean nothing less than that Sweden must look upon itself as a shining example for the world to follow. Maybe not Ronald Reagan's city on the hill, but, well something very much out of the ordinary and worth considering.

By developing real social justice, the Swedes will convert all others, including the politically more or less acceptable, but socially underdeveloped US and the politically unacceptable but socially more progressive Soviet Union.

In other words: the Third Opinion, mega size!

I should add that Swedish leftists who had traveled in the Soviet Union and therefore should have known better labeled the country as socially progressive. Time and time again travelers of that kind claimed that there was no unemployment in Russia although they had seen with their own eyes that this was not at all true. The poverty, enormous and visible to the naked eye, was overlooked. The vulgar and ostentatious wealth of Stalin's new class was admired and enjoyed - the fact that important visitors got most things for free and could change their money at fantastic black market rates undoubtedly played a role.

As late as 1983, Vice Premier Ingvar Carlsson stated that Soviet Communism had indeed succeeded in solving the country's "material problems...." (Only six years later, the empire collapsed, not the least because of its inability to feed and clothe its people.)

The Swedish model never even modestly impressed Stalin, neither did it his successors. That the Americans also went their own way is hardly surprising.

On the other hand, it is important to note that many—and in time all—of the countries of Europe developed in the direction of what came to be called the welfare state. Particularly in Germany where the *Sozialstaat* (the German term) in reality began during the time of the Iron Chancellor, Otto von Bismarck (a sworn enemy of Socialism), the construction of a safety net started decades before the Social Democrats came to power in Sweden. Even if the Swedish politicians hated to admit it, the Germans got to benefit, if that's the word, from even more social protection than the Swedes, who considered themselves world champions. Sometimes it became a bit thick even with the leading socialists themselves. Gunnar Myrdal (a world renowned economist we met in chapter 4) once found fit to complain bitterly:

"We have glorified the Swedish model like we didn't have any history and as if we were alone in the world."

No social scientists have seriously tried to establish why Sweden's Social Democrats became so hostile toward cooperation with Europe—the Europe first known as EEC, later the EC, and now the EU. And maybe no research is needed. The explanation can really only be this: more power to the Union would mean less power for the party ruling Sweden, meaning almost always the Social Democrats.

Power is transferred from the member states to common bodies, mainly the Commission in Brussels; or so one says. There is an element of truth in this, but the reality is considerably more complicated, and looked at from a socialist perspective, very unappetizing.

The Commission is not, as one sometimes hears, the EU government. The commissioners, who are appointed, not elected, can make some decisions, mainly in questions of minor importance. On the contrary, the European Council—presidents and prime ministers from the member countries—decides all major issues. They meet, discuss, compromise, and decide. This means that the big countries, particularly Germany and France, very much run the show. A small country can haggle, complain and sulk, but rarely win.

Or in other words:

Swedish ministers would have to take orders from colleagues who were looked upon as bourgeois (for the last seventy years a prime hate word for the party's supporters). Arne Geijer, the last LO chairman with solid power in both the trade union movement and the party, called, without blushing, the EEC countries' social policies reactionary. This in spite of the fact that he knew well enough that these policies did not differ much from what was practiced in Sweden.

A majority of the Swedes were against what was known as the four K's: Catholicism, Conservatism, Capitalism, and Colonialism (all spelled with a K in Swedish), which mainly shows that knowledge about what the Continent really was concerned with was not very wide spread.

Luckily for the government, the treasured neutrality was always at hand to use as a club against (the rather frail) opposition. Tage Erlander, who better than anyone knew how compromised the neutrality was, did not have to say what he and his fellow party members really thought: namely that we Swedes have done a whole lot better than you down there. We don' t want to cooperate with you because we feel that we are a bit more advanced than you and fear that you will drag us down to your inferior level if we join.... Besides, we don' t want to share power...

Instead Erlander said the following when he spoke to the Metalworkers Union (the most powerful in the country) on August 22, 1961:

"The government has... concluded that membership in the six state association in accordance with the Rome treaty... is impossible without violating the Swedish policy of neutrality."

It should be noted:

1.   That the decision Erlander announced was one of the two most important ones taken during the cold war, and

2.   That the Prime Minister spoke nine days after the construction began on the Berlin Wall (an event Erlander did not see as important enough to warrant even a line in his memoirs).

According to Daniel Viklund, veteran correspondent for *Dagens Ny-*

heter and media's leading expert on the EEC, continental leaders were quite upset. The Swedes were said to be self important and provincial, a sullen and arrogant bunch living on the outskirts of the world, in a country where, as no less an authority than Konrad Adenauer claimed, you could not get a schnapps if you happened to want it at a time of day the authorities deemed unsuitable. (He was quite right.)

Three leading Swedish intellectuals returned the fire from the Continent with a vengeance. In the fall of 1962 a book called "Vi och Västeuropa" (We and Western Europe) was published. It was written by Gunnar Myrdal, Tord Ekström and Roland Pålsson, all three considered leading left of center thinkers. Two quotes will suffice:

"It's the small states… (the citizens) have a higher and more evenly distributed income… they are clean and nice… and have generally arranged their societies in the best manner…"

And:

"..You can venture the generalization that it is largely the Protestant countries that have succeeded in bringing about a reasonably honestly paid income tax. Neither France, nor Italy have succeeded in this respect…"

Views of that kind (quite simply chauvinistic drivel!) were shared by many Swedes, even on the bourgeois side. Indeed, this is still true. But the hostility was worse among Social Democrats and that was the main reason Erlander saw it necessary to close the door as firmly as possible.

What if he hadn't done it?

Sweden would have experienced tougher competition both in politics and business. We would have had a richer and more inspiring public discussion—inspiration instead of navel gazing; we would have been forced to self-criticism instead of self-glorification. And most important: Sweden would have signaled that the country, absolutely and irrevocably, wanted to belong to the democratic brotherhood, what we call the Western World.

On the other hand, it is not likely that the monopoly on power enjoyed by the Social Democratic Party would have lasted as long as it did.

Tage Erlander realized that in 1961. Exactly ten years later Olof Palme came to the same conclusion. The UK had decided to break out of its isolation and to take Denmark in tow on the way to membership. The door was wide open for Sweden, too, but Palme slammed it shut, once more with neutrality as a pretext.

Erlander's speech to the trade union created quite a stir for a couple of weeks but was soon forgotten. That was a pity. No political speech during the 50's and 60's was of anything resembling equal importance. As irrevocable as the war itself, it made Sweden a country of self-selected, arrogant isolation.

We chose to be outsiders.

It must be added that no historian, of note or otherwise, has found reason to visit the archives, interview the participants still alive, and establish *why* Sweden chose this remarkable attitude. Let us think again:

The US, far away on the other side of the Atlantic and shedding a lot of blood because of European crimes and follies, chose to support a unification that made new wars impossible, and slowly but surely created an economic competitor. Sweden, which was saved from slavery under either Germany or the Soviets by the sacrifices of others, including the Americans, refused to cooperate and took its distance until (as the saying goes) there was no longer anybody to be neutral against.

The opposition parties did not protest the neutrality/isolation very loudly. Neither did business. In a typically Swedish way, the CEO's of the great companies, and at the time there were quite a few, saw themselves as globe trotting, profit hungry capitalists, and as public servants of the welfare state. It had been that way for a fairly long time. Ulf af Trolle, who was both a professor and CEO of several companies, described the situation well in his memoirs:

Already before the war there had been a sense of collegiality rather than competition in Swedish business.... The tendency to look inwards increased during the war years when the government welded the nation together with the help of rationing and price control that brought to an end the competition we had had during the 1930's.

Some have claimed that Erlander charmed and cheated the business leaders. I don t think so. The Swedish Capitalists' increasing resemblance to public servants was a gradual process. It is hard to describe, but two chains of events are clearly important:

1. First, many companies made lots of money during the war years, when the state and the Wallenberg brothers essentially ran them. Volvo, which would otherwise have had a very hard time surviving, got all its

research and development costs covered by the taxpayers. SKF (which made the world- famous ball bearings) raked in profits, and many others were almost as lucky. Immediately after the war and for many years to come, Asea conducted its technologically extremely important atomic program in tandem with the state, which also made sure that all important Swedish orders went to Västerås. The banks were by regulations forced to pump so much money into construction projects that not very much was left to entrepreneurship or other adventures; bedsides, it was an unwritten law that the banks' own companies had first call and that it was prohibited to try to win important customers away from other leading banks. In short, the great companies were not socialized but nonetheless dependent on the state to a degree that made it natural for the executives to go for adjustment and minimization of risk, rather than confrontation and chance taking. The CEO and the owners behind him were transformed into administrators and officials. It was no coincidence that the first professional chief of information in the banking world, Toivo Sibirzeff, during many years turned down demands to interview Marcus or Jacob Wallenberg with the words:

That's impossible. He is too busy making money for Sweden.

For Sweden maybe, but not for the family or the companies they owned....

2. Business was good. Swedish products sold themselves, or almost. During the long period of full employment and optimal utilization of capacity, the trade unions (those that had not yet developed into parallel bureaucracies and were not very radical), consistently said yes to new technologies and constant rationalization. Even if the country did not have a business magazine before 1967, businessmen and industrialists got very good press; a great export order was something akin to the national team winning an important soccer match. Under these circumstances it was hardly surprising that the executives liked the situation and saw themselves as extremely capable, and the Swedish system as sound, rational, and productive. Well, the taxes might be a little too high, but for the people at the top there were ways to avoid them....

The fact that the ruling party so clearly said no to the old discredited form of socialization also played a role. Why rock the smooth sailing boat?

Swedish executives were no political animals. Volvo boss Gunnar Engelau was almost certainly not joking when he said that it may be just as well if industry and government—evidently seen as eternally Social Democratic—made their deals without involving the more or less useless opposition parties.

The opposition parties, people said, made trouble and caused unnecessary delays. The government, however, sat down with the business and industry, listened benignly, and decided.

During the 1940's, 50's and 60's, two distinct elites were formed in Sweden. They worked rather smoothly together, not the least because everybody realized that one had everything to gain by not intruding on domains belonging to the other side. Later, a third factor, the media elite, was added, but it was not fully established until the end of the 60's and didn't matter much before that.

The elite that successively attracted all opportunists and a growing number of the country's talented students, we could label the power elite, simply because the common denominator for all members of the group was a lust for power. These people went into what's broadly called government—in other words, politics—where it was a clear advantage to be a moderate Socialist and administration. It should be carefully noted that while Sweden had a great tradition of objective, non political administrators, even at the highest level, this tradition was undermined during the 50's, 60's and particularly thereafter, so that today probably no country has so large a proportion of its administration and key institutions run by political appointees. The present wife of the Prime Minister, Anitra Steen, well known as an insider, has held no less than four posts of the highest importance, notably State Secretary (second in command) at two ministries and chief of the Swedish equivalent of the IRS. She is now CEO for Systembolaget, the giant, state owned liquor monopoly (which we met in Chapter 4). In fact, the power of appointment has been so thoroughly abused that many Swedes today speak despondingly of a one party state; one of the most prominent critics has been Inga-Britt Ahlenius, today's chief accountant at the United Nations in New York.

It should be added that the trade unions, of which the overwhelming majority are run by Social Democrats, contribute to the party's dominance both because of their economic clout and the fact that after the so called reforms in the 70's, they became, in fact, a second tier of management in all Swedish enterprises. Management and trade union bosses very soon developed a cozy relationship, maybe best capsulated in the following exchange:

"Time for a raise," I told the newspaper's CEO.

"I would gladly have given you that," he said, feigning deep sorrow. "But you know, I can' t. The Union wouldn't allow it."

Turned out that the Union was in the midst of a drive to raise only the salaries of the lowest paid employees, excluding all others, a campaign not particularly disliked by the management. Both management and Union bosses generally castigated so-called troublemakers (for which read non-conforming individuals). The playing field shrunk as far as the individual was concerned.

Ordinary Swedes, well aware of the stacking of the administration cadres (which is, if anything, even more prevalent at the municipal level) and the unchecked power of the unions, complain a lot amongst themselves but grin and bear it. They hardly have a chance to do otherwise.

The second elite has its home in business and industry. It is, as it has always been, dominated by a number of big banks: today SEB, Handelsbanken, and Nordea. The first one is a result of a merger between Enskilda Banken and Skandinaviska Banken in the 1970's, still closely associated with the holding company Investor and the Wallenberg Foundation. The most important and commanding owners/managers are two cousins, Marcus and Jacob Wallenberg. Which reminds you that the then Enskilda Banken as well as Investor and the Foundation, were, from before the war up into the seventies, run by two brothers— named Marcus and Jacob. As a sideline, Marcus Wallenberg handled trade negotiations with the British during the war, while Jacob handled the more important Germans. The family had close relations to a number of German trusts and companies and enlisted the help of a high-powered American lawyer. The name: John Foster Dulles, who helped open many doors, not the least when the Swedes during the Cold War wanted to buy arms. Marcus Wallenberg, said US Ambassador Graham Parsons, is no doubt the most powerful man in Sweden. Few would disagree.

The family's power is perhaps not quite what it used to be, but it's still huge. The second big bank is nowadays pretty anonymous, the third, saved by taxpayer money during the crises at the beginning of the 90's, is state owned.

Around the banks, the great and sometimes not so great companies are, as already mentioned, grouped in spheres. Most are thoroughly integrated in the globalized world, not the least since Ford took over Volvo's car division and General Motors Saab's. CEO's and other managers have seen their salaries and perks grow at a considerably faster pace than workers' incomes. It is in Sweden like everywhere else: money talks, everyone else walks.

Well, of course, officially this is vehemently denied.

Swedish trade union density stood at 79% in 2000, compared with 84% in 1994. The three union confederations are the blue-collar Swedish Trade Union Confederation (Landsorganisationen, LO), the white-collar Swedish Confederation of Professional Employees (Tjänstemännens Centralorganisation, TCO) and the graduate Swedish Confederation of Professional Associations (Sveriges Akademikers Centralorganisation, SACO). LO and its 18 affiliated unions had a total of just over 2 million members as at 31 December 2000. TCO and its 18 affiliates had about 1,250,000 members, while SACO had 492,706 members. All figures include non-active members such as students and pensioners.

Source: European Foundation for the Improvement of Living and Working Conditions.

"By the late 1990s the Wallenbergs controlled some 40% of the value of the companies listed on the Swedish stock exchange. Their interests range from Ericsson, a leading telecoms firm, to Astra Zeneca, a pharmaceuticals company now listed in London, Electrolux, a white-goods manufacturer, and ABB, a global engineering giant. After Volkswagen, the family is also the second-biggest shareholder in Sweden's Scania.. There is little that happens in Swedish business that does not involve the Wallenbergs."

The Economist, October, 2006

Until January 1, 2000, the church in Sweden was part of the state. Before the separation, every Swede was born into the Church of Sweden, also known as the State Church. In 1951 the right to leave the church was established; from 1996 you become a member by being baptized. Some 6.8 million Swedes (out of 9 million) are church members, meaning 75.6 percent of the population. However, church attendance is hardly more than 4-5 percent of total membership and most Swedes would prefer to be known as agnostics or outright atheists.

Reformation, meaning change from Catholicism to Lutheranism, came to Sweden in 1593. It then became a crime, punishable by death, to practise Catholicism. Queen Kristina, the daughter of "hero king" Gustaf II Adolf, thus became a traitor to the country she headed, when she converted and left Sweden to take up residence in Rome. No charges were brought and she visited Sweden a few times. Today there are some 84,000 Catholics in Sweden.

The USA became the first secular state in modern times and the separation of state and church has always been total. It is, however, a fact that the USA is, by European standards, a very Christian nation. There are over 300 different Christian churches, 200 Christian TV-stations and networks, and 1,500 radio stations. 9 out of 10 Americans believe in God (if not always the same one) and 28 percent hold that every word in the Bible should be taken literally. Of all congregations, the Catholic Church is the largest in membership (some 33 million) but in recent decades, the so-called Christian Right has grown in importance. One third of the people who voted for George W. Bush in 2000 and 2004, were Christian fundamentalists.

8

Freedom of religion and Swedish promiscuity

As I told earlier, many, if not all of the young Swedish farmhands and servant girls who left for the US were angry with the priests. They often had reason to be. The Swedish clergyman of the day was all too often a harsh and despotic fellow who demanded that the Word of God be followed literally - that is as he (the priest) interpreted it - and who had the full power of the state behind him. In Sweden, since the time of Gustaf Vasa in the 16th century, everybody is born into the Church, and until 1951, one was not allowed to leave it, at least not officially. The state financed the Church and every taxpayer had to contribute, regardless of religion or lack thereof. After 1686, the Church also handled the registry of the population that was required by law in each and every village.

This might sound dull and bureaucratic, but it was in fact very important. The register was made more and more elaborate as time passed. From 1946 it turned increasingly into the service of the tax authorities. (It told if you rented an apartment or owned a house; to report a change of address became mandatory for everybody living in the country. It showed if you were married and if you had children, in or out of wedlock. But first and foremost, the register, which from the beginning of the 1970's has been run by the tax people, gives everyone a number called person number, consisting of year, month, and day of birth, and then a dash with four control numbers. Thus in Sweden the author of this book, but no other person, is known as:

Nilson, Ulf Bertil, 330325-4613. A number of men might share my name (I know of a couple), but no one shares my number.

The last figure is uneven for all men, even for all women. There are, of course, rules for the use of the register, but everyone knows that authorities like the police and sometimes-mysterious commercial interests know almost everything about you. EVERYBODY has a chance to know everybody else's age, income, exact address, and telephone number. To most Swedes, this is not intrusive but a sign of rationality and efficiency. It is considered modern and human, too.

After all, you should not be able to run away without paying for a child you have fathered, should you? And taxes should be paid, should they not? Besides, if you manage to wiggle out of your responsibilities to the collective, everybody else will have to pay more, so let's cheer for the register (and if need be report on each other).

In all this, the Church and the state were always one.

According to the Swedish version of Lutheranism, which was strong (but always on the retreat up to the 60's) if you didn't obey authority promptly and without complaints, you would go to hell. To hell—no ifs, ands, or buts about it! In church this hell was often described almost lustfully as a place where the suffering was unbearable every second, yet eternal, a concept as scary as it is impossible to comprehend. That the priest tried to dominate by scaring the living daylights out of his herd, there is no doubt at all.

A particularly detested feature of religious life was called home interrogation (in Swedish: *Husförhör*). The priest let it be known that he would visit this or that household and ask questions designed to show if the farmer, his wife and children, and the hired help knew their Bibles, their Biblical history, the Gospels, and the Psalms. If somebody stumbled, there was harsh criticism, and of course, the shame, the shame... plus the risk that there would now be no chance of avoiding that hell.

So, there is no reason to believe that the Swedes loved or even liked their priests at the time of the great emigration to the US. Furthermore the man in black was a part of a strict class system with nobility, officials, and as time went on, rich people on top and ordinary folks way down there. In the late 30's, little boys like myself were instructed to step to the side of the road, stand still, and bow our heads when we encountered the priest or the owner of the mill (the richest man in the village). Whoever didn't obey was often reported and got a good whipping for having disobeyed the rules.

The above should not be taken to mean that the Swede in general was not a believer. Some might be uncomfortable and sometimes a bit rebellious, but more against the haughty priest and the system than against Christendom itself. Almost everybody was baptized as a baby, confirmed as a teenager, married in church and buried there. Morning prayers were mandatory in school and the teachers stressed the importance of hard work, prayer, and clean living. The Confirmation was a particularly important milestone. It meant that, after the First Communion, at the age of fifteen, a young man usually got his first watch, his first bike and his first suit with long pants. You could smoke and (sometimes) drink liquor. In other words: after Confirmation you were an adult, a man.

Most people believed in the Father, the Son, and the Holy Spirit. Most knew at least the Gospels (and a lot of hymns) pretty well and most probably said prayers more or less daily. In this there was no difference between the ones that left for the US and the ones that stayed behind.

That, however, would change.

In the US and the colonies that preceded it there was freedom of religion or at least freedom to be a Christian in any way you wanted, from Columbus on. In the beginning the Protestant domination was almost total. Later on the industrial immigration from Italy, Poland, and Ireland made the Catholic Church the largest single religious community.

That there should be no state church in the US was a given. You do not flee from religious persecution only to be forced to worship in a way you might find alien and wrong. Indeed, there might well have been a civil war much earlier if people had not been allowed to build their own churches, sing their own hymns, and actually quite often import their own priests. To be an American was almost inevitably to be a Christian, whether Catholic, fervently Evangelical, more moderate, or perhaps only going through the motions. If you are an American, you belong to a church. Period.

Still, it is important to remember that the US is the first secular state in modern times. In Sweden to be a Christian was for many centuries an inescapable duty; in the US what you believe has always been your own, private business (although, again, it's more or less taken for granted that you do believe in God. In fact, according to the polls, 9 out of 10 Americans do). It is true that the President has always been expected to be a Christian, but the State he leads has no religion. In fact, the three percent plus Americans who are also Muslims are less likely to be persecuted than they were in their countries of origin or for that matter in Europe.

The enormous strength and tolerance of American Christendom can be captured in statistics. As of today Protestants of various kinds make up 63 percent of the population, Catholics 23, other religions 8 percent and no religion 6 percent. There are more than 300 Christian denominations, close to 200 Christian TV-channels and 1,500 Christian radio stations. 60 percent of the population belongs to a Christian congregation and 40 percent go to church every week, as opposed to 12 percent in France and less than 5 in Sweden. 44 percent feel that belief in Jesus is the only road to salvation and 28 percent think that every word in the Bible should be taken literally; 62 percent believe that Jesus will one day come back to Earth.

That Christians do not always keep the peace with other Christians is nothing new and American Christians are no exception to the rule. The Fundamentalists, who have been increasing in numbers over the last decades, are in support of school prayers but against abortions and homosexuals; there is also a sharp division between those who believe in divine creation and those who prefer the Big Bang as well as Darwin. As already said, if the US had not been so Christian a country, it may well have had a second civil war. In my opinion, the main reason this did not happen was because of a man named Martin Luther King and the strong Christian beliefs in the country at large. A short recapitulation:

On the 1st of December 1955, the black seamstress Rosa Parks refused to leave her seat on the bus in Montgomery, Alabama, to a white man. This meant that she broke the law and could be punished. But the law was, of course, unjust and the black people decided to boycott the bus company. King and his friend Ralph Abernathy were elected to lead the fight. It lasted for 381 days and climaxed when white racists blew up King's house. The reaction was violent. Enraged blacks wanted to get arms and take revenge. King spoke to them a speech that was half sermon, half a lesson in political strategy. He managed to prevent the spilling of blood. A short while later the moral pressure on the white community had grown so strong that a court declared segregation on busses illegal: no black person would have to leave his or her seat to a white person. Martin Luther King was celebrated as a hero.

He had studied Gandhi's teachings and listened to his own father's sermons on the supremacy of God and inviolability of human life. But he had also seen black folks bow their heads sheepishly when white men passed by. He had heard black women cry inconsolably when their men had disappeared after meetings by the so-called Knights of the Ku Klux Clan. He knew that black prisoners were routinely beaten up in jails and prisons. He had seen ever more starvation, humiliation, and dirt. His commitment grew and he spoiled for a fight—a fight according to the principle of non-violence. In a famous letter from a prison cell in Birmingham (he was to see the inside of many cells) he stated:

"Non-violent, direct action wants to create such a crisis and such tension that society... is forced to take sides. It wants to dramatize the problem so that it can no longer be ignored."

His greatest victory came precisely in Birmingham, Alabama, one of the most segregated cities in the entire south. In April 1963, he brought out his followers in giant but peaceful demonstrations. Chief of Police Bull Connor met the protesters with clubs and mass arrests, later with dogs and fire hoses. The TV networks went live day after day, while the prisons soon overflowed and the authorities were forced to set up make-shift concentration camps. King increased the provocation by appealing to teenagers, to children. In thousands they took to the streets, were clubbed down, bled, were whipped by violent water beams, got arrested, and sang.

The contrast was unbearable. On the one side were sweaty, well-fed policemen in helmets and dark glasses, revolvers, shotguns, and clubs. The lingo of bars and barracks: Asshole nigger; fuck your mother nigger! On the other side were little girls in white dresses that sang psalms and prostrated themselves in front of their tormentors defenseless and shaking with fear, but indomitable.

Bobby Kennedy, who was Attorney General in his brother's government, asked King to turn down the heat. He refused. After a few weeks, President Kennedy, who was sympathetic to the black cause, but not particularly knowledgeable, could wait no longer. The big Civil Rights Act, which prohibits all legal discrimination, was born. The unholy alliance between Democrats in the south and conservative Republicans in the Midwest blocked it for some time, but a few months after the murder of John F. Kennedy, his successor Lyndon Johnson pushed it through the Congress. (A move that would turn the democratic south republican for some time to come - according to Lyndon's prediction.)

King's fight continued. In the summer of 1963, I stood in the sweltering heat of August and heard him address 200,000 demonstrators in front of the Lincoln Memorial. He was one of the last speakers; the setting sun lit the sky afire and the shadows were lengthening fast. Everybody was tired, many skeptical, but the words made everyone a believer:

"I have a dream this afternoon... The dream that black and white will be able to live side by side, that America can be transformed into a just society." He succeeded in making it sound quite doable, not only a dream, but also a realistic goal. All of us who listened to him believed in his vision, at least right then, simply because of his own strong belief.

That King was later murdered (in the horrible year of 1968) does not change the story. There was a lot of violence, and radical groups like Black

Panthers, Black Muslims, and others gained many adherents. However there is no denying that the fight for Civil Rights is a tremendous success story and that the Christian Church, which grew ever stronger through the 90's, played a leading role.

In Sweden, development took a dramatically different turn. In 1957 the powerful national conference of church leaders decided after many months of acrimonious debate that women could NOT be priests. The Bible, that is to say God, was against it.

The next year the same conference made a 180-degree turn and decided that women could become priests, after all. What had happened? Well, the Parliament had come to the conclusion that equality between the sexes made it impossible to deny women the right to preach and perform other priestly tasks. In other words: the elected politicians, rather than the Church leaders or the believers decided what was the will of God. It was an enormous defeat for the Church or, more precisely, the Church leaders, who did not protest and in fact chose their well paid and secure jobs over their beliefs, thereby bringing down contempt and ridicule on themselves. Indeed, through the years, one more and more often heard the line:

"To become a Bishop in the State Church you don't have to believe in God. But it helps to be a Social Democrat."

The Social Democrats themselves were atheist as a rule. Prime Minister Tage Erlander talked contemptuously about priests as black coats and magicians. That didn't stop him from supporting the state Church at the expense of the free congregations. Some commentators go so far as to claim that there was in reality a silent alliance between the Church and the party leaders. The Church got money and certain privileges in return for *not* being too religious. In return it served as a blocking force against truly Christian and therefore more demanding movements. Typically the Christian groups that were formed outside of the Swedish Church were labeled Free Religious, and had to finance themselves. American churches, among them born again fundamentalists, perhaps some 100,000 of them, often inspired them. However, after 1960 or so, it would be wrong to speak of Sweden as a Christian nation, except nominally so.

And in the 1990's, the fastest growing religion in the country was without doubt Islam, a development much disliked by the man in the street. (See also chapter 13.) Sweden got its American admirers quite early: the columnist Marquis Childs' book, "Sweden: the Middle Way," was a great hit with the liberals in the 30's, and Eleanor Roosevelt herself was quite interested in the Swedish welfare state, of course not the least because her husband's New Deal went in the same direction, however with a very distinct (and all too seldom noted) difference:

In America, welfare in its varying public and private forms was always thought of as something temporary, something to tide you over until you could once more support yourself and your family. For most people it was and is more or less self evident that your way of life depends on what you do and how you do it. Very importantly, it was also seen as something of a duty for well-off people to give money to charities or other worthy causes, such as universities.

In my opinion, in Sweden the system was thought of as a method of permanently upgrading society, making the citizens more and more well behaved and wiser, gratefully looking to the state (that is, the Party) for guidance and direction.

In the US the social engineers broadly thought of individual human beings; in Sweden one saw groups, in other words collectives. In reality, private charity had no place in the system; the argument being that one could not trust that those who gave would continue giving. The State, often called the common—not individual people—should take care of people in need. That way there would be justice and equality.

Or so one thought

Conservatives in America were, for obvious reasons, much less enamored than liberals with the godless, materialistic Socialists in the little country to the north. Maybe that's why a Time article called Sin and Sweden became so much discussed in 1955. The piece stated, without mincing the words, that the Swedes had made birth control, abortions (!), and promiscuity into human rights, which was basically true. Particularly the promiscuity part struck a raw nerve. Was it really true, young (and some older) male visitors asked, was it really true that you only had to ask and then that statuesque, big bosomed blonde would immediately say yes...?

Well, it certainly wasn't true at all. Swedish women could and did say no, much to the consternation of not a few American visitors, particularly young males. In fact, it seems probable that young people in Sweden, the US, and several other countries in the West behaved in quite similar ways but were more or less open about it.

Anyhow, the story about Sweden as a hedonistic society—and an unhappy one to boot—took hold. Another magazine article created a tremendous stir, if mainly because it was quoted by none other than the president himself, Dwight D. Eisenhower. The year was 1960. Ike had read a piece originally published in the *Saturday Evening Post*. He used it when he spoke to republican supporters in Chicago, and since 1960 was an election year, he laid it on thick. Without naming the country by name, he claimed that a socialistic system had led to a dramatically higher suicide rate. I think they used to have fewer (suicides) than almost all other countries in the world. Now they have almost twice as many as we. Also, Ike said, drunkenness had gone up and ambition down. It was, in short, a horrible place.

At first many people thought that the unnamed country was Denmark, but it soon became apparent that Eisenhower had Sweden in mind. Prime Minister Erlander protested, and when Ike was to visit Sweden in 1962 to give a couple of speeches, the US ambassador warned him: the Swedes have long memories; the ex- president might be in for a rough time.

It turned out quite differently. Eisenhower, smiling his sunny smile, confessed that he had been badly informed. He asked every Swede for forgiveness and got it in spades. The visit was a complete success.

It should be added, however, that questions about free sex still abound, whenever I visit the States.

And not without reason.

Since Mr. Eisenhower's visit, Sweden has changed dramatically. Up until the 1970's, divorces were, if not unusual, at least not the norm. Since then one out of two marriages regularly end up in court. At the same time more people than before decide to live together without marrying. The term sambo (cohabitation) entered the language at about the same time and has stayed there. Sambos have in principle the same rights and duties as married people; as far as children are concerned, the rule is that after the divorce, the care and feeding is divided equally between the former partners.

Extremely few Swedes (I personally know of hardly any) consider sex anything but a pleasant pastime. The outbreak of AIDS in the early 1980's brought about an upsurge in the use of condoms, but promiscuity continued to be the rule rather than the exception, and most Swedish teenagers would rather be caught dead than admit that they had not had sex with several different persons. A few, very few, Christian couples might practice abstention rather than prevention and be absolutely faithful in their marriages, but they were looked upon as oddities, perhaps slightly weird. In general the pleasures of the flesh were given free reign.

Nothing illustrated the new attitudes toward love, sex, and children than the abortion question, which is rather, in Sweden, a non-question, as I will explain further on.

In 1944, 134,991 Swedes were born, more than in any other year in history and of course a result of the growing optimism that the war would soon end. That same year 1,088 abortions were performed.

Thirty years later, in 1974, there were 109,874 births and 30,636 abortions.

Another 29 years down the road, in 2003, births had dropped to 99,157 and abortions rose to 34,374. That is, of all pregnancies, more than every fourth ended in abortion, a fact noted in an often-told anecdote:

A young girl calls her doctor:

"I'm going to London for a week, so you have to write a prescription for the pill," she says.

"I can't, it's Sunday."

"So, you want to force me to have an abortion when I come home!"

Many of the pregnant females are teenagers, and some 7,900 a year (or 20 a day) have abortions. Of the young ones, a disproportionate number are immigrants who fear that their parents will feel dishonored by an unwanted and unauthorized pregnancy. Within some communities the punishment for such a break of family rules is death; Sweden, since the early 90's has had its share of honor killings, but more about that in chapter 13.

9

Collision course, the Nixon and Palme years

In the 1970's the US was fighting hard, in Vietnam and within its own borders. The fights were interconnected, which sometimes obscured what was truly at stake.

None of the fights was about Vietnam as such. The Americans, whatever their faults and misapprehensions, were not out to gain real estate. It was as firmly anti colonialist as ever. Neither did it aspire to dominate Southeast Asia, at least not in any totalitarian way. Natural resources were not an issue. The goals were mainly defensive, to stop Communism from expanding (in which it both succeeded and failed) and to tell the world (including the adversaries in Moscow and Beijing) that the US had not gone soft, would not turn the other cheek, and would not leave its friends around the world to fight for themselves.

In this, one was largely successful.

One of the main reasons, maybe even the main reason the war spilled over into domestic political debate was because of Richard M. Nixon.

The war was controversial already under Kennedy, but not yet big enough to engage people outside of what is called the Beltway, the political circles in the capital. The debate grew a good deal more frantic under Lyndon Johnson. LBJ was widely disliked within his own party as well as among Republicans. He sent more than 400,000 fresh soldiers into the battle and became so unpopular that he decided not to run for re- election in 1968 (in spite of the fact that his chances of winning were quite good). Johnson firmly believed that the US must "stay the course", mainly to show the Chinese and the Russians that they had better not dream of world domination or the like; as for himself, he felt that another president had a better chance of uniting the country.

And then came Nixon, the man so many Americans loved to hate, and who, to left wing Democrats, incarnated everything that was wrong with America: too much aggressiveness in world affairs, hysterical anti-Communism, crony Capitalism, and, well, the fact that Nixon was Nixon ("a shifty eyed God damned liar," to quote no less an authority than Harry Truman).

Richard Milhouse Nixon came into office with the heavy baggage of partisanship and personal animosities. He was, in his detractors' words, the accidental president who would never have reached the White House if Kennedy (who beat him by a hair in 1960) had not been assassinated. Nixon was a loser turned winner, only to turn loser again—a dramatic rejection of Scott Fitzgerald's thesis that there are no second acts in American lives.

That the US intervened in Vietnam was hardly surprising, and as already told, at least in the beginning hardly controversial. There is a clear line from the wise men that advised Harry Truman (and helped create NATO) via Eisenhower and Kennedy/LBJ to Nixon and Vietnam. Containment at work—no less, no more. No dominoes were going to be allowed to fall, no costs spared. Nixon, however, decided to change the very framework and thus the very essence of the latest version of the great game.

In the summer of 1971, I was vacationing in Sweden, when the news came in from Washington. After secret trips and involved negotiations, Henry Kissinger and Chou en-Lai (fronting for Mao Zedong) had agreed that Nixon would go to China to meet the Great Helmsman. We, who made our living commenting on world affairs and the Vietnam tragedy, did not miss the point:

There would be a narrowing of differences—in diplomatic verbiage, a rapprochement between the US and China; that much was certain. The risk that the meeting would end in a fiasco was nil. The very fact that the two parties had decided to meet meant that they had also decided that it should succeed.

This would mean a weakening of the Soviet-China alliance, such as it was. The Soviet Union would become relatively weaker, the Chinese relatively stronger.

In other words, the balance of power had shifted. In spite of Vietnam, widely criticized almost everywhere, the US would be in the driver's seat. Some observers even dared to question conventional wisdom and claim that it was really because of the intervention in Southeast Asia that Nixon was able to perform his remarkable power play. Anyway, the leaders in Hanoi became more receptive to the idea of peace, so much more as it was already quite clear that after a decent interval the whole country would be theirs. Henry Kissinger, who on the American side directed the negotiations that began in 1968, pretends (in his book Ending the Vietnam War) that the US really wanted a free, democratic South Vietnam. One is not convinced. Since 1965 it had been all too clear that if the US had not sent in massive forces (543,000 men at the peak), South Vietnam would have collapsed much earlier, possibly already in '65. Democratic it had never been. Neither does it seem that Kissinger's opinion that Laos and Cambodia could have held out until the collapse of Communism in 1989 has any real credibility. Quite simply, the US lost the will to win; Hanoi did not.

Writing about William Westmoreland, who for a long time commanded the US forces in Vietnam, Kissinger states that the general wanted to grind the enemy to pieces with the help of superior technology and resources. In other words: a war of attrition. But, Kissinger admits, such a strategy does not work against an enemy who is prepared to take any number of casualties (particularly not, when one's own side is more and more reluctant to take any casualties at all). But maybe another line from Kissinger's book best sums up the whole affair:

Perhaps no nation has been so uncomfortable with the exercise of vast power as the United States, Kissinger wrote.

Perhaps this has changed. But then again, perhaps it has not.

There is no question that the final outcome of the Vietnam War was influenced, at least in part, by Watergate.

Neither is there any question—strange as this may sound—that Nixon's fall was met not with joy but apprehension and gloomy feelings in Moscow and Beijing. Brezjnev, Mao, and their cohorts saw Nixon first and foremost as an adversary who was, in spite of everything, always in search of that most treasured political commodity: stability. He who wants stability does not try to profit from the problems of others. He is after balance, not turmoil, detente, rather than strife. Since the confrontation over Cuba in the fall of 1962, the relations between the superpowers had stabilized considerably, not the least because of Nixon/Kissinger. The Russians liked it and so did the Chinese (who were still very weak and much more concerned with the Russians, whom Mao hated, than the US, a country Mao really didn't know). Indeed, leaders in both the Communist great powers went out of their way to honor Nixon after the fall—something that could not be said of the countries of Europe and most certainly not Sweden, where he had always been "tricky Dick", the guy you wouldn't buy a used car from.

In the US the debate over Nixon will probably never end. Was Watergate a third-rate burglary or the beginning of a vast conspiracy, which would have snuffed out democracy in the US had it succeeded?

It was, of course, neither. According to a great many people who knew Nixon (and a horde of amateur psychologists), the President never managed to defeat or control his inner demons. He was insecure, therefore brutal and suspicious, well over the borderline to paranoia. He wanted total control and hated nay-sayers. He considered himself persecuted by the eastern establishment, certainly by the liberal media based in New York and Washington. He had a strong sense that he didn't belong to or perhaps rather wasn't accepted in elite circles. Even in the White House he was a loner, a self appointed outsider, sheltered from the world by aids like John Ehrlichman and Bob Haldeman, the "Germans" whose loyalty was uncontested—not infrequently stupidly so.

What is striking when one looks back at the impassioned and politicized time of Nixon is how seldom the word space comes into mind. Yet it seems quite clear that the single most important event in that time was the landing on the moon by astronauts Neil Armstrong and Edwin "Buzz" Aldrin (with roots in Värmland, Sweden) in August of 1969. The successful moon shot was the greatest technological project ever undertaken. It was in a sense a spin-off of the Second World War—Hitler's deadly V 2 rocket—and would likely not have happened as early if there had not been such a fierce race for weapons, scientific superiority, and propaganda gains between the US and the Soviet Union.

The Moon Project itself was of importance for new management techniques, for satellite communications as in satellite TV and satellite telephones, for miniaturization as in cell phones and pocket calculators, and for any number of electronic gadgets, changing people's lives in countless ways. Even more important was the upgrading of computer capacity for the coming of the greatest invention of them all, the Internet. It was begun by the military as a means of assuring fail-safe communications after an atomic attack obliterated one or several American cities and for decades into the future where civilian applications are concerned.

Regardless of all this, on Nixon's watch, for the first time man broke the bonds of gravity and ventured out in the universe. America demonstrated its almost limitless capacity for invention and management, and Armstrong and Aldrin, in their bulky space suits, actually danced on the moon. It gave cause for some celebration, but was actually soon, if not forgotten, at least shunted aside.

Would the same forgetfulness have been the case if John F. Kennedy had still been president when they danced on the moon? Perhaps, but it is hard to believe.

In advance of the election of 1972, which Nixon would have won by a landslide (against the super liberal George McGovern, almost regardless of what he had said or done), the President's men began to play dirty in earnest. Rumors were spread, telephones illegally tapped, dirty tricks performed, and the Democratic Party's headquarters burglarized at Watergate (a fancy Washington apartment complex, not far from the White House).

It is quite unnecessary to go into the details of the Watergate scandal here. Suffice it to say that:

1.   At another time and with another, less hated president, it might not have amounted to very much;

2.   But politics in the years after 1968 were feverish, perhaps not revolutionary (as many participants hoped) but confused, and not seldom, brutal. Young people (and some not so young, like Dr. Spock and Bertrand Russell) were up in arms against their parents, white supremacy, Capitalism, the bourgeois lifestyle (which they enjoyed), and middle class values. You felt but contempt for money. You smoked pot and made love casually, without commitment or care. You walked in demonstrations and called the police pigs. Everybody who wanted to be somebody was up in arms to liberate the Third World, finish the Vietnam War and of course elect George McGovern. When this did not succeed, the next best thing was to support the protest against Nixon. And so it went.

It should be noted, and not only in passing, that Watergate created investigative journalism as we know it today. There had certainly been exposures before (at the beginning long, long ago it was called muckraking), but never before had two young reporters, Carl Bernstein and Bob Woodward, managed to unseat a sitting president. The two showed great skill in using anonymous sources, which abound in Washington, but something akin to genius was naming one of these sources Deep Throat (also the title of a popular movie with the porn queen Linda Lovelace). Who Deep Throat was - or if he or she even existed was not revealed until 2005, when Mark Felt who had been second in command at the FBI, confessed that he had pointed the reporters in the right directions. Considerably more important is, of course, that Bernstein and Woodward became, over a few weeks' time, the gold standard of investigative journalism. All around the world young journalists wanted to expose misdeeds and crooks, the higher up in society or power structure, the better. Somewhat unluckily, the result of the investigation was always decided in advance: if no crime or malfeasance was discovered, no story. The investigative journalist is, for better or worse, always a prosecutor and all too often the leader of an improvised lynch mob.

Was Richard Nixon lynched?

Yes he was, but mainly because he did just about anything to make people forget the good he did (particularly the China trip) and underline his dark and deceitful deeds. Sometimes it almost seemed, at least to an outside observer, that Nixon wanted to be kicked out and dishonored.

Anyway, he was. His successor, Gerald Ford, was but a parenthesis; in 1976 the door opened for two very different populist presidents: Jimmy Carter on the left and, from 1980, Ronald Reagan on the right.

The first part of the 1970's saw the US in agony.

It was not only Vietnam and Watergate. In the fall of 1973 Egypt, Syria, and Iraq suddenly attacked Israel. For some strange reason the Israelis were not prepared. The attack began during the Yom Kippur holiday and for a few days, the survival of the Jewish state hung in the balance. The superpowers, the US and the Soviet Union, sent threatening signals, but apart from supplying their respective clients did nothing hostile. In the end the Israelis got the upper hand, mainly because of a brilliant attack across the Suez Canal directed by Ariel Sharon. A truce was negotiated, skillfully brokered by Henry Kissinger; in due course it led to Anwar Sadat's visit to Jerusalem and an historic peace.

The oil exporting countries in OPEC took the occasion to unsheathe for the first time the oil weapon. Prices kicked skyward and both the US and Europe came close to panic as long lines formed at gas stations and inflation curves pointed dramatically north. In the US, Nixon, very much against both his instincts and his beliefs, imposed price controls and cut loose the dollar from gold. This meant that the US currency was left to float, leaving it to the market to decide its value against other currencies. Float in this case meant sink: in effect the US devalued.

So did Sweden, repeatedly, in the 1970's. Swedish consumers were forced to pay more for imported products, while the vital export industry could offer better prices, make better profits and (if only theoretically) create more jobs. Indeed, Sweden became a devaluation country; international bankers looked at the Krona with suspicion; Swedes in general, however, didn't much care.

Jimmy Carter, after his ascension to the presidency in 1977, alienated the Russians, who had been quite comfortable with Nixon. Carter preached human rights and supported dissent: anathema to the old men in the Kremlin. More important is perhaps that Carter could not quite seem to inspire Americans. He was too pedantic, too nit picking, indeed too cold. He seemed, at times, to claim a special relationship with God and a corresponding contempt of all adversaries.

"I'm going to talk to God about this," he once told Senator Howard Baker.

"Well, when you're in there, tell Him that I'm concerned, too," Baker replied.

It must also be said that Carter had bad luck. A little more than two years after his inauguration, in January 1979, the Shah of Iran was toppled by a popular uprising, brought about and directed by Muslim imam. The most powerful leader, Ayatollah Ruhollah Khomeini, who had spent many years in exile, returned from Paris and quickly made himself the absolute ruler of the country. All presumptive contenders were ruthlessly executed every morning. Tehran's newspapers were filled with portraits of the preceding night's victims and every mullah in the country preached hatred against supporters of the Shah, Israel, and of course, that Great Satan, the United States. Women were directed to wear the chador, covering everything except the eyes; movies and music were banned and so was liquor. Men were supposed to wear beards. Tehran had never exactly been a fun city. Now it became, if you were not a true believer, a nightmare (although we, the traveling reporters who were there, soon found out that the black market functioned well, especially when it came to liqueur).

The ayatollahs added insult to injury by letting a loosely put together band of students attack and occupy the US Embassy in the central part of the sprawling capital. Some 400 diplomats were held as hostages for almost a year (333 days) and not allowed to leave before January 20, 1981; the day Ronald Reagan succeeded Jimmy Carter.

Realizing that the ongoing crisis, which ABC's Nightline highlighted continuously, would seriously hurt his chances of reelection, Carter arranged an operation to remove the hostages by force. The attempt failed dismally when helicopters crashed into each other in the desert staging area, leading to an abort and total fiasco. Carter also hurt himself considerably by speaking of a "malaise" in the country, perhaps the last thing Americans wanted to hear.

As if the loss of Iran wasn't enough, Carter could do nothing but look on when the Russians invaded Afghanistan towards the end of 1979. He did call for and got higher defense spending, but the increase took a while to take effect (and was generally credited to Ronald Reagan).

It should be noted that one of the leaders of the students in Iran, a certain Mahmoud Ahmadinejad, was towards the end of 2005 elected president of Iran. Shortly after his election Ahmadinejad called for the destruction of Israel; there was every indication that the country was well on its way to producing nuclear weapons.

Olof Palme's foreign policy was, seen with hindsight, not only wrong-headed, but quite strange—maybe because it was in reality much more domestic than foreign. As already told, Sweden said NO to Europe and NO to NATO, but yes to just about every revolutionary regime and so called liberation front you could find. The little yellow men that attacked, killed their enemies, and then disappeared back into the jungle became heroes not only to impressionable youths, but also indeed to the Prime Minister himself (who in his efforts to co-opt more extreme leftists became rather extreme himself).

The times were aflame and the debate sometimes quite senseless. A well-known economist, Bo Södersten, in his book published in 1970 claimed that the legendary Father of the Country, Per Albin Hansson would probably have liked Fidel Castro. "It is hard to believe that he would have taken his distance from the efforts... to let people who normally live apart work side by side in jobs strange to them but for a common goal." As for myself, I think that Per Albin, who preferred a middle class lifestyle, would have said a distinct no if invited to swing a machete at Fidel's side in the sugar harvest. Södersten himself got his ideological purity brutally questioned when, four years later, he tried to get an article critical of Salvador Allende published in the party's ideological periodical Tiden. The piece was refused, in spite of the fact that Södersten was a leading member of the editorial board. Neither were Swedish newspapers keen on reporting that Allende won the election with only 36 percent of the votes.

Arthur Lundkvist had moved quite effortlessly from The Third Opinion to cultural radicalism, which is basically the same thing. In an enthusiastic book "Så lever Kuba" (How Cuba lives), Lundkvist wrote:

"He is the new Cuba's indefatigable schoolmaster, speaking pedagogically, interested in everything, working almost all hours, present nearly everywhere.... When he harvests sugar cane he breaks all records... He has elected himself leader and the people have confirmed his choice... it is a great luck for Cuba to have a so youthful, adaptable, honest and humanly inclined leader..."

In this nonsense, Palme's close aide, Pierre Schori (who would become both Under Secretary for Foreign Affairs and a cabinet minister) concurred. As late as 1986 (when 10 percent of the Cuban population had fled the country). Schori claimed that Fidel not only belongs on the list of the greatest men in contemporary history (yes, he really said that!) but also that he reminded one of a renaissance prince.

And so on and so on in the spirit that would lead famous author Per-Olof Enqvist as well as politician Birgitta Dahl (later on Speaker of Parliament in the democratic country of Sweden) to salute the dictator Pol Pot, who presided over the killing of perhaps 2 million of his country men. To be radical was equal to being in favor of freedom, progress, and justice. Conservative or liberal was to be racist, defender of genocide, reactionary, and in favor of corrupt privileges.

That's the way it was. To many in the indistinct group known as radicals, Palme was a bit on the tame side, but most looked up to him anyway or at least thought that he was the best man available. This impression was strongly reinforced when, in February of 1968, he walked in a torch lit parade alongside the ambassador of North Vietnam.

The manifestation was reported all around the world and drew quite a lot of criticism, not the least from Americans. Palme defended himself in the parliament where he appeared as angry and insulted as people who knew him expected to be. On the other hand NOBODY had expected a totally new analysis of the world situation. Palme said:

"...since a monolithic aggressive Eastern bloc quite clearly does no longer exist, many have chosen to see an aggressive Chinese nationalism as the foremost threat...."

A few months after the speech, Soviet tanks rolled into Prague. The Eastern bloc might not have been monolithic, but it was certainly not totally un-aggressive.

Year in and year out, this did not stop Palme from strengthening his criticism of the US, his more or less contemptuous opinion of Europe, and his love for the Third World. And the Soviet Union? For domestic political reasons Palme's supporters always stressed that one of the most important underpinnings of Sweden's neutrality was that the country would serve as a bridge builder, a creator of contacts and an honest broker. Some supporters went as far as to claim that when Palme, while temporarily out of power was made chairman of a UN sponsored commission on disarmament, the US and the Soviet Union hardly spoke to each other. This was a blatant lie. The two big ones negotiated in many different forums, not the least about strategic weapons. Foreign initiatives were NOT invited and it was an open secret that both powers encouraged mutual satellite surveillance, discreetly tipped each other off concerning movement of troops, and always always emphasized that the other one was special. Palme knew this full well, but chose to go with the (uninformed and biased) flow.

Besides, the Americans disliked Palme and showed it by never inviting him to Washington and never arranging a meeting with the president—a meeting Palme wanted very much indeed.

Leonid Brezjnev in Moscow did invite Palme and treated Sweden cordially, albeit lukewarm.

The quite frequent intrusions of Soviet submarines in the Swedish archipelago, revealed under the right of center coalition government between 1976 and 1982, was a problem one decided to downplay. Typical is a protest note in April of 1983. It said:

"The security situation in Northern Europe has for decades been marked by low military tension and stability. To preserve this situation it is required that the great powers show restraint in their military actions..." Palme, in other words, protested against violations by the Soviets by demanding that the US should show equal restraint, a demand that probably made the old men in the Kremlin smile contemptuously...

In his First of May speech 1984, Palme used up 51 lines of his manuscript (notes biographer Bertil Östergren) on the situation in Latin America, essentially an attack on the US. The Soviet invasion of Afghanistan got one (!) line. A short time later the book "*Svensk utrikespolitik*" (Sweden's foreign policy) contained 82 lines filled with attacks on the US, still Central America, mainly Nicaragua, but two lines on Afghanistan and Sweden's neighbor Poland. The

The Soviet Union was not mentioned.

The American distaste of Palme began with the torch lit parade. The Prime Minister himself was elated and happily told (eyes characteristically aflame) that pictures from the parade were published in 367 American newspapers. On the other side of the Atlantic one was n o t amused and the irritation continued to grow. The day before Christmas Eve 1972 Palme protested against American B- 52's bombing Hanoi.

"One should call things by their right names," he said. "What goes on in Vietnam today is a form of torture. There can be no military motives for the bombings."

Until then, the US leaders, including Nixon and Kissinger, would probably only have yawned; considerably worse things were said closer to home. But Palme continued:

"Because of that the bombings are an evil deed. There are many of those in modern history. They are often tied to names such as Guernica, Oradour, Babij Jar, Katyn, Lidicie, Sharpville, and Treblinka. Violence has triumphed."

The US reacted violently, mainly because Palme had used the name Treblinka, one of Hitler's extermination camps. Henry Kissinger, being Jewish, was particularly enraged and the Swedish Ambassador Hubert de Besche, was instructed to report home that Washington had never noted that Sweden protested with equal strength against anything Nazi Germany did before or during the Second World War, a not so subtle way of hinting at cowardice and opportunism.

Palme's reply was a conciliatory letter to Nixon, but in reality his decision to steer Sweden along the radical way hardened. The small country should gain weight and influence by allying itself to countries in the Third World and stake out a new route: the Third Way, the Third Opinion between the two power blocs. In the states that had earlier been colonies there was a need to pursue such a line and Palme quickly became quite popular. Of equal importance is the fact that the project was enthusiastically received also at home. Foreign policy is domestic policy in all countries, but more so in an isolated place like Sweden. Many intellectuals were, as already shown, overwhelmingly enthusiastic. As Ann-Sofi Nilsson wrote in her book "Den moraliska stormakten" (The Moral Great Power), "a man and his time found each other... Palme, better than most, was able to adapt himself to the ideological and intellectual climate of the day."

Well, maybe a better description would be: to use the ideological and intellectual climate for his own goals. This is quite legitimate. In democratic politics you have got to be elected, after all! But it is important to point out a decisive flaw in Palme's and his supporters' reasoning, a policy that made the US and the Soviet Union equal, favored dictatorships and one-party states. If only they claimed to be socialist or work for liberation, such a policy precluded a clear and uncompromising commitment to democracy. In its place we got what is known in Swedish as *kålsuparteorin*, an expression impossible to translate but meaning something akin to plague on both your houses, a policy that to be meaningful must mean taking distance from the US as well as the Soviet Union. In June of 1974, Palme explained:

" One of the super powers is organized as a hard capitalist society… The social problems are great… There is a glaring contrast between its outside power and its inability to solve internal social problems… Its ideals have been badly corrupted in Vietnam… The other super power represents… a perversion of socialism… It is a system that has gone stale in dogmatism and bureaucracy… Demands for freedom are met by skepticism and doubt, if worst comes to worst, with tanks…"

In the party program of 1975 the same thoughts were further developed. The plague on both your houses became official Swedish policy. The Third Way, the Third World, the Third Opinion!

"The rapid increase in production in the capitalist world leads to a steady increase in the detachment of large groups from the labor market. Capitalism is unable to stop the creation of mass unemployment and rising inflation… In large parts of the world, feudalism and private capitalism have been replaced by societies where private ownership of means of production has been denied. The change has meant that in many cases the citizens have achieved a well-being that was unthinkable during the old regimes."

As everybody knows it would have been much more honest to write that some citizens would score important gains. That is to say those who were willing to become lackeys to rulers like Castro, Phan van Dong, Julius Nyerere, Daniel Ortega, Miguel de la Madrid, and a few others in the exotic group favored by Palme.

The man had found his time and his fellow travelers and even Swedish media persons who should have known better (I plead guilty here) hailed him as a great international statesman, which he certainly was not.

Much worse is that the concrete policy that followed placed Sweden very close to the Soviet camp. As Sweden's pre-eminent expert on international affairs, Ingemar Dörfer, has written, this was particularly serious in connection with NATO's so called double decision in 1979 and the following basing of the Pershing and Tomahawk missiles in Western Europe, mainly Germany, in the fall of 83. The background:

After the Cuban crises of 1962, when the Russians felt humiliated, they began a crash program to gain nuclear superiority in Europe, and helped by this decouple (meaning scare away) the US from its allies in NATO. Quite soon SS-20 missiles with three warheads each were pointed against several large European cities, reportedly including Stockholm. The theory was that the Americans would never sacrifice Washington for Frankfurt and that a growing Soviet superiority would lead to greater influence and maybe a Finlandization of the whole continent. Quite simply, the old NATO slogan: the US in, the Germans down, the Russians out, would be replaced by US out, Soviet in.

After cries of alarm from German Social Democratic leader Helmut Schmidt, one of the first to understand the gravity of the situation, the Western powers decided to counter the Soviet move by also rearming. Moscow appealed to the so-called Peace Movement in Europe (in Russia, of course, it was banned or state directed). The crisis deepened and in Germany the NATO line prevailed first after a dramatic speech in the Bundestag by another leading Social Democrat, Francois Mitterrand of France, who, when the chips were down, had very little love for the Third Opinion.

Palme and Sweden's government on the other hand were strongly and openly critical of NATO, lamented the basing of the missiles, and painted scenarios implying that the US, not the Soviets, was dragging the world towards nuclear war. The Soviet Union at the time had 729 missiles in place. The US had 0.

The Peace Movement and Sweden (Dörfer writes) wanted the match to finish 729-0. Ultimately, the negotiations that started after the basing of the Pershings and Tomahawks led to the abolishment of all middle distance missiles. In other words: 0-0.

Equally important is of course to understand that 1983 was the year when the world turned. The evil empire started to come apart, in part because of Ronald Reagan's decision, announced on the 23rd of March, to launch the Strategic Defense Initiative (SDI or Star Wars). A few days earlier, the President had branded the Soviet Union as the "Evil Empire". The men in the Kremlin were quite shaken and when the basing of the missiles came, there was a quiet panic. Indeed, there are some reports that the Russians at least toyed with the idea of a preventive war.

Anyway, it is no exaggeration to say that the US and NATO won the Cold War in 1983 and did so not the least because the US had a president who said what he believed and believed what he said.

In this context, however, it's more important to note that Sweden, which is to say Palme and his successors, particularly Sten Andersson, did not contribute to the victory. They went off to show more understanding of the Kremlin than the enslaved people in (for example) Estonia, Latvia, and Lithuania. Palme saw to it that Sweden became world champion when it came to condemning distant (and often erroneously perceived) injustices. Closer to home, the country was marginalized, and on the wrong side.

Another three facts must be stressed:

1.   The right of center governments of 1976-82 followed basically the same policy as Palme, albeit with a lower profile. There was no intention to apply for membership in NATO and absolutely no enthusiasm for Europe.

2.   The so called Palme Commission, sponsored by the UN and active from 1980-82, finally got its act together and published a report labeled Common Security. It was of course praised in Sweden but was really obsolete before it was published; in three important works on nuclear questions published years later, it is not mentioned.

3.   The UN appointed Palme as mediator in the Iraq-Iran War. It was a hopeless task. The war went on killing and maiming thousands and thousands of people until both countries were bled dry and could go on no longer. By that time Palme had been dead for two years.

Palme's analysis of the world situation was wrong all around. He saw Vietnam as victorious. It was not. Hanoi's victory led to more people being enslaved. The real victors in Asia were Japan, South Korea, Singapore, Hong Kong, and other countries who, DURING THE TIME THE WAR WENT ON, modernized, went over to market economy and (more or less) democracy. Capitalism, which Palme detested, won by a knockout. Witness 1978, when Deng Xiaoping turned Mao Zedong's economic policy 180 degrees, and furthermore 1991, when the Soviet Union collapsed.

In the same way, it was wrong to see Sweden as a happily irresponsible balloon floating over the world, rather than one trying to anchor the country in the solid and democratic European Community. I believe, of course without being able to prove it, that pure vanity played a role here. Sweden's leaders, not the least Palme, rather wanted to be singularly important in Managua or Dar-es-Salaam than one of many in Brussels. Rather a red carpet in New Dehli than a place in the line up outside the White House. And worst of all: even if Palme always said no to Communism, he was absolutely committed to what he called socialism or solidarity, meaning that the elite and the social engineers decide and common folks obey.

His foreign policy was crazy; there is no other word. It was a fiasco. That it did not lead to a tragedy for Sweden is due to the fact that the balance of terror, which he detested, had made Europe a relatively un-dangerous place.

Even for neutralists like him.

10

Olof Palme and the pitfalls of cradle to grave security

I have criticized Olof Palme's foreign policy harshly. I am sure that most Swedes do not agree with my assessment. They will experience my words as an attack on the country itself, which they are not. Neither will they agree with my opinions on what happened in domestic politics up to Palme's death in 1986 and after that tragic event.

Maybe this is only natural. After all, who likes the national team to lose?

In 1998, Swedish industrialist Jan Stenbeck, shuttling between Stockholm and New York, asked me to study Sweden's development from the early 1930's and to write a book about it. I did. The book was given the name "*Sverige: Sluten anstalt*" (roughly: Sweden, Closed Institution, as in penal institution), meaning that the Swedes had become inward looking, not to say narcissistic; a mental fence had been built to keep the outside world at a safe distance. Paradoxically, while globalization continued full speed and Sweden became more dependent than ever before on people, events, decisions, and markets far from its shores, the people showed less and less interest in everything that could be labeled foreign. The reason, I think, is poorly hidden fear: What if we are not the best, after all…?

I worked hard on the book for a little more than a year. Jan and his aides had no input whatsoever, but were satisfied, even enthusiastic, with the manuscript. Then a funny thing happened.

None of the big publishing houses wanted to have anything to do with the book. I had earlier been published by all of them and a few books had gone over quite well, but now they all said no. The most honest one (chief for a house associated with the employers' federation) said simply:

"If there is criticism of the Wallenberg family (which indeed there was) we are not going to touch it."

On the other side of the political divide another publisher was equally firm:

"Your criticism is too harsh. You simply can't say the things you are saying about Palme and much less about the system! One simply doesn't say those things."

I became angry and decided to go it alone. With the help of a friend in the IT business, I put the book on the Web. It was downloaded by almost 15,000 Swedes in the first two months, a very high number for a nonfiction work (which normally sells around 3,000 if successful). Encouraged by this we produced a print- on-demand paperback edition that sold quite well, too, and still does. The story I told was basically the following:

Palme.

No other Swede in our time has created equally strong emotions, at home or abroad. I don't like the old cliché that you loved him or hated him, but that is pretty much the way it was, if with the difference that you could love and hate Palme more than once in the same day. His great charm and genuine kindness made you leave a meeting feeling strongly positive only to discover a little bit later that you thought his politics abominable. He was a one hundred percent political animal, always out to convince, cajole, and control. He was also temperamental, thin-skinned and prepared to charge his opponents with evil and treacherous schemes; he once even spoke of political adversaries as "evil in a Biblical sense".

What did he mean?

Well, I guess nobody knows, but Palme was extremely skilled with words and expressions. He was fast on the draw but never shot from the hip. He would never have spoken of evil in a Biblical sense if he had not wanted to develop a picture of the person he was out to hurt as a creature of dark and sinister forces. Thorbjörn Fälldin was dishonest, Gösta Bohman a disgusting devil, and so on. Palme's eyes were aflame, his fists in the air; he was a master at pausing in mid sentence to give a biting line time to fester and hurt. He was himself and played himself, which is not unusual among great men. He never allowed himself to show uncertainty, at least not outside the inner circle of devoted followers. Just the same I came to believe that deep down, he was VERY insecure. Palme, who was seen as a visionary politician, in reality lacked a bearing vision—a fact that stands out when you look at what he achieved as opposed to what his admirers claim he achieved. His problem was (I guess) that he knew he wanted power but did not really know what to use it for; he was, in that sense, empty.

I was never a political reporter in Sweden, but I covered Palme during a couple of election campaigns and followed him around the world when he was chairman of the UN Commission on Disarmament. We jogged together around the Imperial Palace in Tokyo (where a jogging Prime Minister was as common a sight as a calf with six heads) and in Ayatollah Khomeini's Teheran, where the big-bellied bodyguards were close to fainting as they tried to follow us.

We were neither friends nor enemies, and I don't claim to have known him well. Who, after all, did? Just the same, I managed to be deeply impressed by his professionalism, known to all, and his vulnerability, which was considerably less known. Even when we had not met for a longer period of time, he somehow managed to steer the conversation towards the fact that my father had been a true proletarian, first a stone cutter, then a functionary in the stone workers unimportant little trade union. It was evident that Palme found this very important. The reason, of course, can only be one: I belonged to the working class, while he, born in a noble family, only represented it.

"Your dad was a stonecutter," I remember him saying. It probably meant that he found me a bit weird, perhaps treasonous, because in spite of my background, I clearly did not vote Social Democratic.

Some time before Palme's last election, the so-called Harvard affair exploded. It turned out that Palme had given a lecture at the perhaps most famous of American universities. He had been paid $5,000 in the form of financial aid to his son who was a Harvard student. Palme had not declared the income in his tax returns and was therefore, without doubt, guilty of tax evasion (one of the few crimes where punishment is tougher in Sweden than in the USA).

I wrote about the affair in a column in *Expressen*, pressed the case rather hard and predicted that the episode would hurt the Social Democrats in the run up to the election. A couple of days after the column had been published, I met the once and future Prime Minister on Lilla Nygatan in the center of Stockholm, casually and without any kind of security detail, walking towards his last election rally in the Humlegården park.

When he saw me he rushed across the street, blocked my way and stared straight into my eyes. "You wrote…" he said, or rather shouted, "should I have taken all the money?"

He went on with something to the effect that if youngsters like his son would not be able to do scientific research, Sweden would decline as a nation. Calming down he went on to state that the criticism I had directed at his opponent Ulf Adelsohn, was quite correct.

A bit shaken, it took me a while to realize that Palme had actually confessed, at least indirectly, his tax evasion. At the time, I only noted that a group of Italian tourists filmed us, evidently shocked by finding themselves in a country where the Prime Minister saw fit to attack a citizen walking peacefully in the Old City.

At a gathering of Swedish industrialists in 1968, Finance Minister Gunnar Sträng, a legend in his own time, concluded that Sweden no longer needed many reforms; society was almost completed as far as social reforms are concerned. He couldn't have been more wrong. Palme and the other young leaders who took over from Tage Erlander, who was old and tired in 1969, wanted reforms in workplaces, schools, and peoples' homes; there should be a more just distribution of income and wealth, more collective decisions in all walks of life. Sweden should be a society of equality where everybody should be, maybe not as equal as the Chinese under Mao (that would be too far!) but certainly more equal than Swedes had ever been. Of course, the equality had to cover gender too—it is from the beginning of the 1970's that feminists start to more or less criminalize women who want to stay at home with their toddlers, rather than leave them in nurseries.

The long and short of it was that life should be arranged for everybody and directed by politicians, backed up by "experts". Politicians of all kinds dressed the enormous transformation that was to come in different verbal clichés. Life should be made better for the many, the under privileged, the lowly paid, families with children, people who need care and, for that matter, common folks.

That financial equality is impossible without high marginal taxes was understood and applauded.

Almost all politicians, media figures, and other savants saw the wave of the future as centralism, collectivism, and the elimination of income differences: policies geared to limit the freedom of the individual in favor of the common good. Palme's biographer, Bertil Östergren noted perceptively that the Prime Minister always favored collective decision making (which he saw as more democratic) over private decision making. The old king, Gustaf VI Adolf saw the same tendency and found the ruling party as rather intoxicated by power. He feared (totally without foundation, it turned out) that the days of Monarchy were counted and the Crown Prince would never become king.

In short you could say that Palme and his supporters wanted to socialize not the enterprises, although there was an attempt in that direction too, but the citizens. A quick glance at the most important laws that were passed in Palme's days shows how ruthlessly (in the clinical meaning of the word) one worked to make individuals conform to a society where directing functionaries made as many decisions as possible. All facets of life were regulated to make private choice unnecessary or impossible.

In 1969 pensions were raised. In 1971 Sweden got a 40-hour work-week. The same year the tax code was changed in a way that changed Sweden so fundamentally that no planner, however skilled, could have predicted it. Before the change, husband and wife were taxed as if they had one income, which was therefore comparatively high and highly taxed. Now, both incomes were taxed separately, which meant that it became quite a bit more attractive for women to work outside of the home.

The result was a deluge of women from homes flowing into the labor markets broader and faster than in any other country. The fact that most of the women were employed in nursing and health care increased the need for tax money as well as the need for more caretakers. It also increased the need for children's nurseries to be provided by the community and protected from both competition and dissenting ideas.

The daily migration from home to nursery to place of work and back still goes on. How fast it developed is best told by figures. In 1973, when it was still acceptable to be a homemaker, 16 percent of the children between 3 and 6 years of age went to a nursery. In 1989 the figure was 64 percent. In 1970 some 50 percent of all mothers with small children were homemakers, by 1990 only 14 percent. In his book "*Det tomma rummet*" (The Empty Room), liberal politician (and sometime Consul General in New York) Olle Wästberg concluded:

"During the 1970's, it became in reality impossible for most families to live on one income. But to be able to have two there must be child-care."

The liberation of women (as the reform was labeled) became, if you look at it from another angle rather a command: You must do like all the others, leave your kids at the nursery and go to work. Critics noted scathingly that:

"Instead of staying at home and taking care of her own children it became mandatory for a woman to work in a nursery, taking care of the children of other folks…"

For many years there was very little opposition to what amounted to a rather drastic reorganization of family life. Today, this has changed. About a third of Sweden's 290 municipalities have instituted or are discussing the institution of a child care subsidy to be paid to mothers who decide to stay at home with their kids, at least for the first and perhaps second year. The Social Democrats are four square against the change; the Moderate Conservatives are for it, as are the Christian Democrats.

The next year, 1972, the most important decision made it possible for somebody who seemed unable to find a job to be (in literal translation) retired before his time—in other words, paid by the state for ever, no questions asked. The number of retirees grew very fast. In the 1990's Sweden had almost half a million early retirees; at this writing there are 565,000—more than 6 percent of the total population. Some Swedes have actually been sent into retirement at the age of 20 and without ever having held a job. Of the 565,000 more than 100,000 are said to be alcoholics, although that statistic is not very precise.

The year of the first oil crisis, 1973, brought dental insurance, parent insurance, and unemployment insurance. The next year saw the oil crisis worsening. There were long lines at the gas stations and a lot of bankruptcies, but the Swedes ploughed on and passed a law making it next to impossible to fire anybody. Which, of course, made workers feel more secure and employers reluctant to hire. Palme called the reform the most important thing that had happened since the right to vote was granted.

In 1974 part of the Constitution was changed, giving the Prime Minister a more presidential role.

In 1975, laws were passed about (among other things) pensions, education, and support for adult studies. But much more important is the fact that it was in 1975 that Rudolf Meidner, born in Germany, famed economist who worked for the central trade union organization, LO, presented his proposal for the so-called Wage Earners Funds. By forcing all companies, barring very small ones, to pay part of their earnings into special funds run by the workers' representatives (another way of saying trade union officials!), the power over trade and industry would successively pass from the capitalists to "the people".

The proposal drew fierce, not to say hateful criticism. It no doubt helped the opposition to victory in the next election year. Sweden was lucky, for if Palme had prevailed, the Wage Earners Fund, as nightmarish a construction as you could imagine, would probably have come to pass. Sweden would have gone completely socialist and, I dare say, to hell. Whoever thinks I exaggerate should remember that 1975 was the year the US was forced to leave Vietnam - remember the helicopters on the embassy roof! Revolution seemed the wave of the future and Palme never missed a chance to rail against Capitalism and multinational companies, be they Swedish or American. The Social Democrats, according to Marita Ulvskog (who would become party secretary), felt the center-right election victory was a coup d'etat.

Sweden devalued itself out of inflationary crisis in 1971, 73, 77 (twice) and 1981 and 82; the last time, with the Social Democrats back in power, it was a whopping 16 percent. It went the same way in October 1992 when the krona was allowed to float and immediately sunk by almost 30 percent. All in all, Sweden exported unemployment and imported profit for the export industry.

But back to the 1970's.

In 1976, retirement age was reduced to 65 years of age. However, it is important to note that so many were pensioned off before their time that retirement occurred on the average at the age of 59, which happens to be quite in line with most European countries.

The next year, 1977, the biggest change occurred when a law with the acronym MBL was passed. MBL means that the employees are to have a big say in the running of the enterprises. The representatives, who are, of course, the trade union representatives, are to sit on the boards and must be consulted on matters big and small. Indeed, the union became a parallel power structure even inside the companies. The employers soon learned to use the situation. In most places, the trade union chairman or woman was given a better job, a nicer company car, and so on. This undoubtedly made them more pliant when, for instance, one wanted to fire a "troublemaker" or close down an unprofitable section.

As earlier mentioned, I experienced the new system personally, when, in the early 1980's, I asked for a raise. The CEO, who was my good friend, waxed sympathetic and said:

"I would have been so happy to oblige, but you know, the Union has decided that all raises have to go to the lowest paid."

Finish palaver. Even observers quite close to the trade union movement began to think that maybe the central organization, the LO, had become too powerful—in reality, a government on top of the government.

1978 saw laws about five weeks paid vacation; prolonged parents insurance, better work environment. More important was a law that, at least in practice, gave the HRF (the big tenants association, strongly allied to the Social Democrats) the right to negotiate rent levels. The same year the trade unions became principals of the unemployment insurance corporation.

Unemployment compensation used to be paid by workers cooperatives, financed by contributions from the members. Now, the state took over the financing, at the same time as the unions kept the right to decide over the giant sums of money involved. As for the individual, he or she was more and more dependent on the state and municipality administration, the unions, the associations and the officials. In other words: the system.

In 1980 men and women were made equal by law. More important was the law that made it the explicit duty of the municipalities to support all citizens who were not able to support themselves. The law was, as is often the case, not very clearly written. However, it came to be interpreted as giving any family or individual the right to lodging, TV, telephone and of course food and clothing, as well as health care and schools for the children. The so-called welfare cases certainly did not live lives of luxury and leisure, but neither did they fare worse than the working poor. Sometimes better.

All the new laws changed the country profoundly. Interacting with global developments and changing market forces, it created what we could call a state of functionaries in so far that fewer people work for private companies than work for the state and the municipalities or are dependent on support from these institutions.

Between 1960 and the early 90's, employment in agriculture and forestry declined by 350,000 jobs—a whopping 79 percent. Industry shrank even more dramatically. Trade, on the other hand, thrived and doubled its employment. The end result however was that private employment decreased by some 300,000 jobs, a considerable amount in a country where the amount of people of working age is around 5 million.

What the numbers mean is that reality changed, and for tens of thousands of people no doubt for the better. Sweden got better health care and better services for the elderly, better nurseries and so on, all valuable, well meaning, and not very politically controversial. It was like people in the small isolated country high up north had come up with a way of making gold out of stone. Or so it seemed when one listened to the politicians or the commentators who admired them. (*Den ville jag ge guld och diamanter som skördat stenar där han gått med plog...* "He, who harvested rocks with his plow is the person I'd like to offer gold and diamonds..." From "The thinking rural postman"—*Den tänkande lantbrevbäraren* by Hjalmar Gullberg.)

Not only that. Nobody can deny that a public sector can produce good things. If a sick person is cured, he can work again and pay taxes. Children who are taken away from parents addicted to narcotics or alcohol to live in foster homes might have a better chance of escaping a life in crime. And so on.

That the enormous expansion of the public sector hurt Sweden therefore was not due to the fact that the jobs created were artificial. They were not. On the other hand they unbalanced the economy and depleted morality by being too expensive, too many, and most importantly, by making the clients passive. Three points are essential:

1.   Nobody seriously denies that high taxes are a bad thing and the expansion of the public sector forced the highest taxes in the world upon the Swedes. To become rich or even moderately well off by working and saving became impossible. Taxes became so high that tens of thousands working Swedes could not make ends meet without subsidies that had to be decided on, checked, and administered. Inevitably, cheating and working the black market became a national pastime.

2.   These giant, all-encompassing systems are notoriously inefficient. As leading economist Klas Eklund has shown, productivity in the public sectors has fallen successively, meaning they are employing and paying more workers to do the same job earlier performed by fewer. In the 1990's primary education was twice as expensive per pupil as in the 60's. There were no signs at all that the quality of education had improved in a corresponding manner.

3.   If there is a giant health care system, there simply must be many people needing care. If not, one has to scale down and fire workers; and, as far as health care is concerned, that mainly refers to the women that had just more or less been forced to work outside the home..

Without sick people, no hospitals. Neither public nor private clinics for alcoholics would survive without the drinkers. For this reason it is not altogether certain that nurses or psychologists feel sad when say Sven comes back for treatment for the seventh time. It is, after all, a question of jobs, namely the jobs of those who support themselves by taking care of Sven. Or less provocatively said: if you let people know that there are subsidies for both this and that it will be 1) more common to look for subsidies, and 2) more tempting to legislate new systems for transferring income from those who work to people who, for various reasons, do not work. Definition of the word duty becomes fuzzier, while the definition of the word entitled is sharpened. That one had to support oneself was more or less a religious duty in Sweden all through the 1950's and 60's, but in Olof Palme's days we had a paradigm shift. The Society took over and we landed in an induced helplessness. In his book "When There is no More Money" (*När pengarna är slut*) author and commentator Anders Isacsson writes:

"The real problem with the policies of welfare and security, the cancer, that destroys the system from the inside, is… the citizens' rational adjustment to the supply of subsidies… The system simply generates its own demand, more of the same all the time: welfare produces clients, assurance against injuries in the workplace produces injuries… the refugee policy refugees, the ability to retire before retirement age, people who retire early." And so it goes.

To give the reader an idea of the comprehensive nature of what I call the System, I know of no better way than quoting some basic figures on employment and dependency in Sweden.

Employment and dependency in Sweden:

Working in private enterprise	2,532,163
For the municipalities	873,891
For regional authorities	250,835
For the State	227,280
Total employment	3,874,169
Whereof in the public sector	1,352,006 (Or 34 percent)
Old age retired	1,600,000
Pensioners before old age	565,000

Total of persons dependent on state or municipalities for salaries or subsidies 3,517,006

To which it must be added that all Swedish children, regardless of need, receive a monthly payment to help pay for (already subsidized) nursery school and other costs. Millions of working families also receive a rental subsidy, without which they sometimes would have to downsize their dwellings; needless to say handouts of this kind do not make people more independent or eager to question the system.

In the US, you elect a person, be it for president, senator, congressman, public prosecutor or dogcatcher. All candidates must make themselves known to the voters, try to convince or charm them (or both) and, when elected, see to it that they are credited with delivering on their promises. After the primaries, two candidates generally fight each other, one Republican, one Democrat, but always two faces, two different persons to like or dislike, to trust or find wanting. In the end one of the two concedes, in most cases gracefully, and the winner takes it all.

Any voter (or for that matter non-voter) can call or write to, fax or e-mail their congressman or congresswomen and most will receive a reply. Americans, if they like, get to know their leaders personally, and media helps a great deal by noting voting habits, irregular campaign contributions, and connections among the high and mighty. And so on.

Swedes, on the contrary, do not vote for a person but for a party. The importance of this could hardly be overstated. Almost no Swede knows the name of his or her member of parliament, much less whether he or she is competent. Politics has long since become administration; politicians are technocrats, albeit often without the education or experience of a good technocrat. The candidates for the respective parties, which receive cash subsidies in proportion to seats in parliament, are selected not in the open, but in the proverbial smoke filled rooms (where nobody smokes nowadays).

The party leaders generally decide who is to go to the top of the list and who will languish on the downside without the slightest chance of being elected. Hard and anonymous work in the party apparatus is regularly rewarded; to follow the party line is a sacred duty and to say that the system resembles the Soviet Union in its glory days is to say the obvious, even if the dictatorship of the party leaders is neither bloody nor brutal. The fact that all the parties are constructed in basically the same way makes for a numbing sameness, a lack of drama, and a steady -as -you -go mentality totally at odds with the glamour and razzmatazz of US politics.

Disgusted Center Party politician Dick Erixon summed it all up pretty well after the 1998 election. He wrote:

"The …center right parties act as if they are a part of the political power. That is the most important explanation why they have never in modern times had real power and never will… Not even in government have they done anything but applied Social Democratic policies with Social Democratic values..." Young conservative activist Gunnar Strömmer put the same thought even more provocatively. The election in 1998, he wrote, was a competition between 7 Social Democratic parties.

Someone once said that "Sweden is a such small country—there is only room for one opinion."

Well, not too far from the mark...

In the year 1900 the USA was #3 on the list of countries with the highest GDP per capita. Sweden came in #13.

Fifty years later the USA was # 1, Sweden # 7.

In 2006, the USA checked in at # 7 with Sweden at #8. According to NationMaster.com, the US GDP per capita was $39.453, Sweden's $38.481.

11

In the US, Silicon valley and the internet; In Sweden, the rise and fall of a family empire

While Sweden was busy building its particular kind of velvet Social-ism and political debate in the US was focused on the war in Vietnam and (on the left at least) the evilness of Nixon, the world was changing in ways nobody had been able to predict. With the benefit of hindsight, what happened in the Pentagon, at a few American universities, and along the part of California that was to be known as Silicon Valley, was more important than anything that happened in politics.

Of course, the ground had been seeded. In this context, three years are particularly noteworthy.

In 1954, Stanford University in Palo Alto ran into financial problems. It was decided to try to remedy the situation by creating an industrial park, where companies that so wished could rent space. One of the first takers was an outfit run by William Hewlett and David Packard, found-ers of a coming world power in computing (and both future billionaires, of course).

In 1957 the first Sputnik was launched. It suddenly appeared that the Soviet Union was on its way to winning the space race. And worse, rockets with the power to put a payload in outer space also had the capability to carry a nuclear warhead from, say, Moscow to Washington. Sputnik meant that   the balance of terror was beginning to shift in the Russians' favor. In the election campaign in 1960, John F. Kennedy was to use the phrase missile gap to good effect (that it actually didn't exist didn't matter very much).

In 1962, after much discussion and hand wringing, Paul Baren of the Rand Corporation (a think tank close to the US Air Force) got the job to create a system that made it possible to maintain command and control even after a major city had been destroyed in a nuclear attack. In other words: an A-bomb destroys Chicago. All communications from and to the city are lost. But military information is routed via alternate tracks around the disaster area and is instantaneously available at the appropriate headquarters around the country. Six years later, Baren's work resulted in the ARPANET. The acronym stands for Advanced Research Projects Agency; more importantly it became the forerunner of the World Wide Web. As operations started in 1968, four universities were included in the operation, three of them in California.

At about the same time, two young men named Bob Noyce and Gordon Moore tired of their jobs at Fairchild Co. They wanted to run their own business - a company they called Intel - and set out for the Valley. There they completed the development of the first single chip microprocessor in 1971, the very year the name Silicon Valley was first used in a trade journal. Noyce, who was a very convincing fellow as well as one of the creators of the loose and easy Californian management style, wrote a one page memo to venture capitalist Art Rock. Rock read it once and proceeded to come up with 2.5 million dollars in two days. The race for smaller, faster, more powerful computers was on in earnest. So was the race into venture capitalism, which grew exponentially over the next decades. Intel, of course, was on its way to becoming the world power it is today.

The same year, Alan Shugart of IBM constructed the first floppy desk and a year later ARPANET introduced the first e-mail program, still totally unknown to everybody outside the inner circles. In 1974 the word Internet is used for the first time. That no similar activity was detected in the Soviet Union or elsewhere in the East Bloc should surprise nobody; in a country where it is prohibited to own a typewriter, communications are not a priority. Indeed, the Russians did their utmost to stop the spread of ideas, not to encourage it. As for Sweden, it simply did not have the resources, the market, or the will to take big risks. What Swedish industry did instead, I'll tell a little further on in this chapter.

Even in the US there were at the time no efforts to combine the fledgling computer industry and the Internet on a mass basis. But the day was fast approaching when the computer would be everyman's tool and the Web everybody's playground, library and preferred arena of expression.

In 1976, Steve Jobs and his buddy Steven Wozniak put together the first Apple computer in Jobs' parents' garage. It was, looked at with today's eyes, a cumbersome and clumsy machine, but it had two great advantages: it was user friendly and it didn't cost much. (The first unit

140

sold for $666.66 because Wozniak had a telephone number like that.) Apple became an overnight success and Jobs, as visionary as he was thin skinned and difficult to work with, went on to become one of the most important industrialists of the twentieth century.

The same, of course, must be said of Bill Gates, who founded Microsoft in 1981 and released the first version of Windows four years later, when he was already well on his way to becoming the richest man in the world, treated as a statesman of the highest order whether he visited in Beijing, London, Stockholm, or Washington, D.C. At that time companies like Netscape, Dell, Cisco, and Oracle were also in operation and well on their way to greatness and becoming household words.

To round out the very brief history of how the world changed, just three more items:

In 1983, the Domain Name System was created at the University of Wisconsin. That way one was not forced to remember numbers.

In 1990, a European, the Englishman Tim Berners-Lee, working for CERN, came up with the Internet's language, html, which he decided should be available for free use by everybody, not just internally at CERN (the European Organization for Nuclear Research).

In 1992, the World Wide Web was established and www.com soon became part of everybody's language.

More than 99 percent of it happened in America. It happened because of entrepreneurial spirit, a willingness to take risks (and fail and start all over again), and on the part of the public (which we sometimes call the Market), to try and adapt to new tools, gadgets, and methods. Change and hard work are both integral parts of the American Dream, without which there would never have been a Silicon Valley and never an Internet.

If Steve Jobs had been born in Södertälje, south of Stockholm, he would probably still be tooling in his parents' garage and be seen as slightly weird. Or maybe he would have switched to a job in the municipal government, where he could shuffle papers all his life without running the risk of being fired—nor of getting rich.

Regardless of that, Sweden's economy, not the least the industrial part of it, landed in a trap during the 1970's. It was in a way quite understandable. Many of the country's grand enterprises, like telephone giant Ericsson, go back to the late 19th century. With slight exaggeration it could be said that the domestic market was always too small for the companies. They simply had to first export and then, quite soon thereafter, establish themselves abroad. In the case of Ericsson, the Nobel brothers (who actually started in oil) and a few others, the first important country was Russia. Long before the expressions came in use, the Swedes were both multinational and global. As far as is known, only Holland has more global enterprises than Sweden.

From 1870 all the way into the 1970's, Sweden's economy grew without interruption. The expansion was unprecedented. We were best in the world, economic historian Bo Södersten claimed. Such a fantastic development could not fail to leave its mark on Swedish mentality. We Swedes at this time saw ourselves as the chosen people. Nothing could harm us… when the 70's arrived with stagflation and international depression, we were less well prepared… than any other country.

Once more, this is quite understandable. Sweden made great money when Hitler started to rearm Germany in the 1930's. The Germans bought all iron ore LKAB could produce, all ball bearings SKF cared to make, and many other products as well. When the war came, competing companies in other European countries were bombed, lost workers to the armies and, in general, lost the power to compete.

When peace finally came, things got even better for Sweden. The enormous need for cars, bicycles, kitchen machines, and radios, as well as machines, tools, construction material, etc. made almost everything easy to sell. The only really limiting factor was lack of skilled labor, which was solved by importing workers (see chapter 13). The Marshall Plan helped a lot by pumping dollars into the system and greasing trade connections, much to Sweden's advantage.

Then came the Korean War, which gave the boom a new life. No wonder Swedish CEO's and their advisers, living, after all, in a pretty isolated place, came to think that all that was needed was to expand production and sell more and more of the same. In the 1960's when competition began to strengthen, one realized that one had to improve the products and this was duly done. But more important was what was not done. Sweden produced no new products—that was left to mainly Japanese and American companies. A dramatic example is what happened with the very successful office machine concern Facit. As early as 1963, its boss, Gunnar Ericsson, a low key, immaculately dressed, well meaning executive, came back from a trip to Japan and announced:

"The pinwheel calculator is history. It will not be able to compete with the Japanese electronic calculators."

Ericsson was absolutely right. But unluckily for him and Facit, he didn't act as if he believed his own analysis. Facit actually increased its production of mechanical calculators, built new factories, and expanded its sales force. Swedish quality would win the day, one thought, in spite of the fact that the electronic calculator cost less than a tenth of the mechanical one, was much easier to use, and therefore made the user more productive. Many other Swedish companies acted in the same way. User- friendliness was hardly yet a notion in the US, much less in more traditional Sweden, where the engineer, not the marketing or sales person, was king.

The outcome was inevitable. In 1972 Facit was bleeding profusely. To avoid bankruptcy, the company was sold to Electrolux and disappeared. But that was only the beginning.

The 1970's also saw the disappearance of just about all of the Swedish textile industry. Labor costs were too high to compete with Italy, Portugal, and later on Asian and eastern European countries. The government tried to relocate some production to the northernmost part of the country, always hard hit by unemployment, but the costs were just as high as in other parts; the experiment failed dismally, as everyone should have known it would. Politics played a great and negative role all along. After 1976 a center/right coalition got a chance to rule the country. The bourgeois leaders were dead scared to appear less worker-friendly than the socialists and therefore made it their business to save jobs at all costs. In other words, they subsidized industries that were failing so that they could go on, producing at a loss while paying workers who should have done something else. Many other European governments have gone the same route but seldom with the same misplaced enthusiasm as Sweden, where the forces of the market are often perceived as brutal and evil.

The famed Swedish shipbuilders became another example of the protection of failure. Sweden had several big, internationally renowned shipyards, among which Götaverken, Eriksberg, Lindholmen, all in Göteborg, and Kockums in Malmö, were the best known. All were hit by first furiously growing competition from Japan and South Korea, then by the oil crisis, which resulted in smaller consumption and consequently smaller need for shipping. The way the government reacted was typically Swedish. The shipyards would be bailed out by tax money to be able to keep up production of ships nobody wanted to buy! And employment. Many experts hailed this as a sound decision, for if the ship workers did not work, they would have to be paid unemployment compensation!

Very important to remember is that the center/right government that came to power in 1976 was even more eager than the Social Democrats to aid the shipyards. Billions of kronor were paid as subsidies to the companies that were nationalized under the name Svenska Varv (Swedish Shipyards). Indeed the most successful socializer in Swedish history was Nils G. Åsling, who belonged to the Center party and served as Minister of Industry. Dr. Åsling's emergency room, as his ministry became known, doled out billions upon billions, getting ownership in return; ownerships, that is, of dying enterprises.

In 1970 the combined shipyards employed 22,000 people, plus several thousands more working for suppliers of various kinds. Two decades later total employment was 3,300, all building smaller crafts, mainly pleasure boats.

All the big shipyards were gone (one is now a museum). Together with them the proud and historical steel industry almost disappeared. Just like the shipbuilders they were taken over by Dr. Åsling. The previous owners were compensated. The workers were not.

Since Volvo was founded in 1927, no new Swedish company has grown to become a big employer in the home country. The explanation for this can be summarized as follows.

First, as already stated, the home market is too small. To survive at all, Swedish enterprises of any size must export, which more and more means to establish production abroad, closer to the customers. During the same years that the public sector was built up to its present size, employing tens of thousands of Swedes, industrial employment actually shrunk (see the preceding chapter). But that is only half of the story. Industrial employment in Swedish companies shrunk inside of the country but rose abroad. In 1979 total industrial employment in the big Swedish concerns was 759,338, of which 315,398 worked abroad; 58 percent were Swedes, 42 foreigners. When we come to 1987, which is the year Swedish workers became a minority in Swedish companies, 51 percent of the work force is employed outside of the country. Today, many of the famous companies, such as Volvo, have twice as many employees abroad as at home. Or maybe one should say home, for in reality most of Swedish industry is

- located outside Sweden;

- run by foreigners;

- owned by foreigners, not the least of which are American funds;

- dependent on foreign customers.

As the saying goes, the great companies left but forgot to bring the Swedes with them. That might be a facetious commentary, but the truth is that Volvo, once the very symbol of Swedish success, is today a truck company while the car division is owned by Ford... just like Saab is one hundred percent General Motors. Asea became ABB with headquarters in Switzerland, Astra went abroad and so did the forestry concern Stora (the world's oldest stockholding company), which was bought by the Finns. Foreigners—Germans and Americans and Finns—own two of the country's three leading and totally dominant energy producers, E.ON and Fortum respectively. The third and largest, Vattenfall is state owned but creates as much of its revenue in Germany and Poland as in Sweden. The story of how things have changed is also told by a listing of the ten biggest companies, by the number of employees. They are: The Post Office, Volvo Trucks, Ericsson, Samhall (state owned, established to create jobs for handicapped people), Volvo Cars, Scania Vabis Trucks, TeliaSonera (formerly the state telephone monopoly), Apoteket (the state pharmacy monopoly), Praktikertjänst (an organization of private doctors and dentists), and Skanska (construction).

The story of how Sweden's industry became less and less Swedish is also the story of the disappearance of all the great financial and industrialist families except one: the Wallenbergs.

As noted in chapter 3, the cornerstone of the family's influence (and wealth) is a tax-exempt foundation, Knut and Alice Wallenbergs Stiftelse. The foundation owns great chunks of shares in most of the country's leading companies. Besides, the members of the family managed to collect not only money, but also connections, in Sweden and internationally. The older Marcus Wallenberg was well known in business circles all over Europe, and his two sons, Marcus and Jacob soon became international stars. In Sweden they were admired and feared, maybe more feared than admired, even if nobody dared say so openly until both were gone. Stora's CEO for many years, Bo Berggren, summed it up neatly when he said:

"In contacts with Marcus Wallenberg there was always an element of fear involved."

It should be added that Wallenberg—less discreet than his older brother, whom he didn't like—behaved like the dictator he really was. He thought nothing of calling his CEO's, often very powerful men themselves, at three o' clock in the morning to bawl them out or tell them to stand by only not to call again.

"Isn't it remarkable," I once told one of MW's closest aides, "that the old man casts such a shadow?"

The man was silent for a while. Then he smiled weakly and said,

"Well, if it only were a shadow…"

In fact, the brothers did the country invaluable service, particularly during the Second World War and after.

The government of Per Albin Hansson was not very well versed in foreign affairs. Few cabinet ministers spoke any foreign language (in schools, German was taught as the first second language until after the war when it was replaced by English), and very few had traveled or studied international politics. It was therefore quite natural to look for help from the private sector.

Which meant the Wallenbergs.

A deal was made. Marcus Wallenberg would handle trade negotiations with the allies, while his brother Jacob would take on the Germans. In reality they were to negotiate the same thing: Sweden's trade with Germany.

Sweden needed coal, coke, iron, shipbuilding material and many other things. Germany was no less dependent than Sweden. First and foremost it needed iron ore from LKAB and Grängesberg to make canons, tanks, airplanes, grenades and battle ships. Famed diplomat, Gunnar Hägglöf, could write:

"The trade between Germany and Sweden was in volume one of the most important in the world…" It was the most important in Europe. In 1937, 21 percent of Sweden's imports originated in Germany. In 1940 it reached 40 percent and in 1941 almost 70! The allied nations were deeply unhappy about this. Churchill produced several murderous plans, but the fact was that Kiruna, where the ore was extracted, was very, very far up in the north. To attack it with positive results was almost impossible. Besides, acts of war would perhaps have drawn Sweden into the war on the side of Germany, and who needed that?

So, Jacob Wallenberg negotiated, while his brother kept the British reasonably happy. It must be noted that Jacob in fact represented not only Sweden, but also himself. How so? Well, the negotiations dealt with which company would deliver what and at which price. Many of the companies belonged to what was called the Wallenberg sphere and many others did business with them. So there was plenty of room for Wallenberg to favor his enterprises at the same time as he, undoubtedly, helped Sweden. When I did a study of the books used in Swedish schools I found no mention of any of this, not even that Germany was Sweden's largest trading partner.

But it gets worse.

A book published in 1986 by two Dutch researchers, Gerard Aalders and Cees Wiebes, revealed that in the beginning of the war, but before the US entered it, Enskilda Banken bought the electronic giant Bosch's American company, ABC. This was done to make ABC Swedish and therefore free to do business. But Jacob Wallenberg, who performed the transaction on the Swedish side, was but a puppet. Between him and Bosch there was an agreement that Bosch could buy back ABC when times got better. Prime Minister Per Albin Hansson knew about the agreement.

Enskilda (which means the Wallenbergs) helped the German company IG Farben in a similar way and made a lot of money doing so. Farben, it should be noted, produced the gas Zyclone B, used in Hitler's camps to kill the Jews. Enskilda also gave big credits to a Norwegian company named Norsk Hydro, which produced heavy water (used in the construction of atomic bombs!) and aluminum. Before the war, Marcus Wallenberg was chairman of Hydro.

After the war, Wallenberg risked for a short while to be blacklisted in the USA. But charges were dropped, maybe not the least because one of the investigating lawyers, a long-time friend of the Wallenberg family, was named John Foster Dulles, later Secretary of State and immensely powerful during the Eisenhower years.

During the Cold War, Marcus Wallenberg used his connections in both government and business in the US to facilitate the buying of arms. It is fair to say that several generations of Saab's fighter-bombers would never have flown without American equipment.

The two Dutchmen's book was, dare I say, of course never published in Sweden. Nor do Swedish history books, as I have already stated, tell boys and girls how one rich and powerful family became almost a state within the state, and therefore even more rich and powerful, able to tower over all others.

After Marcus Wallenberg's death in 1982, the power of the family has shrunk somewhat. His anointed successor, Marc, took his own life in the

1970's and his brother Peter, while powerful enough, didn't quite match his father's performance. The same could be said for the group's two current leaders, the two cousins named (what else?), Marcus and Jacob.

Important facts leading to the erosion of the family's power are internationalization and changing ownership. When the first Marcus and Jacob ran the show, most Swedish companies were almost totally owned by Swedes. Today, foreigners own more than 40 percent of the shares listed on the Stockholm Stock Exchange.

The days of the fenced in family farm are over.

In Sweden 10,435 companies owned by foreigners operated in 2005, meaning that one fourth of all Swedes working in the private sector of the economy had foreign bosses.

Swedes owned assets worth SEK 6,700 billion (around $1,000 billion), while foreigners owned assets worth SEK 6,963 billion in Sweden.

During the last fifty years, the working age population has increased by around 1 million. The number of men and women employed by private enterprises remains the same as in 1960.

The average Swede pays SEK 6.8 million in taxes during his or her lifetime. He/she gets 5.6 back in the form of various subsidies. Statistically a Swede has to live to the age of 87 to get back all that has been paid in to the state.

12

Immigration. The Swedish vs. the American way.

When I was a young man in the 1950's, I had never seen a black person. Well, fighters like Joe Louis (and later on Floyd Patterson) were pictured in the papers and in the movies; of course, one met colored singers and servants. But in real life: no. Maybe you could find a couple of what were then called Negroes in Stockholm or Gothenburg, but not in the part of the country where I lived.

If anybody had predicted that less than five decades later Sweden would be a country where 20 percent - one out of every five - was an immigrant, he or she would have been laughed right out of the room. In fact it was hardly before the end of the 1960's that one began to note foreigners. But here we are today: one out of every five people living in Sweden was born abroad or is the child of somebody born abroad. (Note that a child born in Sweden of non-Swedish parents does not automatically become a citizen.)

Of course, foreigners did settle in Sweden earlier, even before Sweden actually became Sweden. In the Middle Ages, the great trading organization, the Hanseatic League, operating out of ports in primarily the northern part of what was to become Germany, sent representatives to Stockholm. They did much to teach the Swedes how to trade, and for a while German was the business language in Stockholm.

Merchants and sometimes adventurers soon followed the Hanseatic people from the countries around the Baltic, which was to become in the 17th century more or less a Swedish lake. Stockholm was at the time a leading city and therefore one of the area's magnets.

With Sweden established as a great power, another wave of immigrants came. Sweden, being at the time (see Chapter 2) the mightiest military power in the world, needed officers and other experts and officials. Many noble families from the Baltic countries Germany and Poland chose to settle in the country. Quite a few of them left to make war in the countries they came from. Armies were multinational enterprises at that time and officers were generally of noble birth.

When iron and steel industries became important for the new great power, capital, competence, and skilled labor were all imported, most notably from what is now Belgium. Among others, one thousand skilled men were handpicked to work in factories founded by Willem de Besche and Louis de Geer, both very prominent among Sweden's early industrialists, both from the area around the city of Liege. Both became Swedish; their descendants still live in the country. It is well known, but nowadays not very often mentioned, that Sweden would not have been able to sustain its great power position as long as it did without the foreigners.

After Finland was lost in 1809, Finns, many for whom Swedish was the mother tongue, came to settle in Sweden. Immigration from other countries slowed to a trickle. No longer a great power, Sweden was not as attractive as before; instead the great wave of emigration started, and between 1845 and 1925 the country lost over one million people, almost all to the US. Today over 4 million Americans claim Swedish decent, although many of them are at the same time German, British, Estonian, Spanish, Italian, etc.

During and after World War II, tens of thousands of refugees came to Sweden, in spite of the fact that they were not particularly welcome. Most actually returned to their countries of origin when the hostilities ended. Jews were a special case. Sweden shamefully encouraged the Germans to stamp Jewish passports with a J so that they could more easily be denied entrance. However, as the war went on and Hitler's Wehrmacht started to lose, Sweden became more generous, and after the capitulation many Jews were allowed into the country.

As earlier told, Swedish industry after the war went from success to success, not the least because everybody in most of Europe needed just about everything and Sweden was one of the few countries with its production capacity intact. This meant that more workers were needed, workers that were simply not available inside the country. Import of people, particularly industrial workers, became necessary. In 1954 an agreement was signed creating a common labor market for the Scandinavian countries; again many Finns decided to leave their war-ravaged country and settle in much richer Sweden. Later on, during the 1950's and 60's, workers from Italy, Yugoslavia, Greece, Turkey, Czechoslovakia, Hungary, and a few other countries arrived. On principle all who came were guaranteed a job, mainly in big industrial companies like Asea, Elextrolux, Volvo and so on; the overwhelming majority adjusted very well and was gradually and without problems assimilated into Swedish life.

Then the problems started.

The newest immigrants started to come in the fall of 1973, after the military coup that overthrew Salvador Allende in Chile. The Chileans, of whom many were socialists, had every reason to fear for their lives in the home country, where Augusto Pinochet and his henchmen established a bloody, military dictatorship. The Swedes had been extremely positive to the Allende regime, thinking its brand of Socialism was the beginning of great change in Latin America. The refugees were warmly welcomed and were granted asylum without difficulties. This meant, among other things, that the news soon spread around the world that Sweden was soft on refugees and generous with staying permits.

And so it was.

All through the 1970's and 80's asylum seekers trickled in. One of the largest groups came from Iran where the Ayatollah Khomeini took power in 1979, meaning that everybody who did not wish to live under fundamentalist Islamic rules had better get out or risk prison or death. Also many Kurds chose Sweden, because they felt persecuted in Iran, Iraq, Turkey or Syria. A large number of Lebanese citizens (very often Palestinians) fled the civil war that had started in 1976; quite a few returned but fled again when Israel attacked in 1982; the process was repeated in 2006.

Then, in the beginning of the 1990's the pace quickened. Somalia collapsed (and gave the expression failed state a contemporary and frightening face). Refugees spread all over the world and many came to Sweden, where they were met the same way as all other asylum seekers.

First, they were asked to present their passports and/or other identity papers. This most had learned to expect, so they had thrown the papers away or sometimes flushed them down the toilet on the ferry ship from Germany or Denmark. This, it was supposed, made it easier to claim that one came from a town or village occupied by unfriendly forces, that indeed, to be sent back meant death.

Second, the Somalis, who were usually without the skills needed in the Swedish labor market, were sent to camps, usually well built and quite comfortable, to await a decision: will they be allowed to stay or not? The refugees got money for food, and medical care was available free of cost; maybe not surprisingly, many Swedes grumbled that foreigners (like criminals in prisons) were treated better than elderly Swedes having to make do on meager pensions.

Third, the deciding authority, called *Utlänningsnämnden* (the Foreigners' Committee) proceeded to investigate each and every case individually, according to law. Realistically (as I wrote many times during the 90's) this was a hopeless task. Even a well trained and experienced journalist with good financial resources would have a very hard time establishing if Hassan or Dilsa really came from this or that particular village in Kurdistan. And were their lives really threatened if they went back? Were they not in fact economic refugees and therefore not in need of asylum?

It would be impossible to establish the truth even if one traveled to the area and spent a long time there, searching for documents and interviewing people, I wrote. For bureaucrats working out of offices in Sweden, there was no chance at all.

Worse still, the decision to refuse asylum, which was handed down with great regularity, could be appealed, quite often several times.

It all meant (and still means) that the foreigners had to stay in camps, totally dependent and totally passive for up to four years; the average time being around two. After that a few were sent home, while thousands, in a stunning turnaround, were granted permanent staying permits (the Swedish answer to the Green Card) for humanitarian reasons. The immigrants were then helped to housing, but much more seldom to jobs, and could start calling for relatives to come to Sweden. About half the immigrants from the last twenty years or so are in fact relatives, quite often elderly, of people who got to stay for humanitarian reasons.

During the early 1990's the immigration rose to record levels with the country's population growing fast, exclusively because of foreigners; Swedish women (of the old kind) statistically produced only 1.49 children each, way below the replacement level of 2.1. The newcomers were mainly Bosnians, Albanians from the Serbian province of Kosovo, some Croats and yet more Kurds, Somalis, and Iranians. Almost all were Muslims and several mosques were built but no churches. The years 1993 and 94 stand out. In 1993, 61,872 foreigners were admitted; in 1984, no less than 83,598 were admitted, which meant that the population grew by almost a full percentage point in that year alone. Another revealing statistic tells us that the number of gainfully employed Swedes, aged 16 to 64, declined from 83 percent in 1990 to 72 percent in 1999, a net loss of 420,000 jobs. During the same years the country took in 350,000 asylum seekers. More than 90 percent could not prove that they risked torture or death if they were sent back. Legally they had no right to asylum, but were given permanent residence permits for humanitarian reasons.

The enormous influx of foreigners was brought about mainly by the small, Liberal Party (*Folkpartiet*) with the help of its partners in a short-lived center/right coalition government. In spite of the dramatic change, the country suddenly filled with alien and alienated people; there was really no political debate. The establishment, both in politics and media, decided that to criticize immigration amounted to being racist and hostile to strangers. A small party called New Democracy (*Ny Demokrati*) managed to gain several seats in parliament, mainly because it did offer some criticism. But it was mercilessly attacked from both left and right and soon collapsed. Immigration became a non-issue in spite of the fact that the newcomers worked less, demanded more subsidies, and committed more crimes, particularly rape, than what was called, for lack of a better term, ordinary Swedes. The editor of the evening paper *Expressen* was summarily fired after he dared publish an opinion poll saying that a majority of the Swedes would love to see the newcomers return home. A number of books written by quite responsible and well-qualified researchers were refused by all major publishing houses and even ignored by the media. A strange kind of self-censorship demanded, and got, silence.

And yet, people started to question what was going on. The Liberal Party suddenly discovered what just about everyone else knew: that there were more and more slum areas in Swedish cities. A report, published by the party, called The Map of Alienation, told that in 1990 there were 3 very problematic areas in the big cities. In 2002 one found 136! Not only Stockholm, Göteborg, and Malmö, but scores of smaller cities reported grave problems; in Malmö, where immigrants constituted 40 percent of the population, ethnic youth gangs fight running battles every night and a researcher from the University of Lund recently reported that young, Muslim men raped Swedish women, because they want to make war on the Swedish society. In other words, a creeping, civil war, brought about by race, religion and sex. Strong words, grave comments indeed—and most certainly true.

Just the same, the news was duly reported by media, but under small headlines, and soon forgotten. Neither did anyone find it truly sensational that the name most often given newly born boys in Malmö nowadays is Muhammad.

Sweden is, no doubt, one of the healthiest countries on earth. It has been that way a long time. In fact all the time since 1840 the average life expectancy at birth has increased with 2.5 years per decade. Both men and women in Sweden can today expect to live well into their 80's, in most cases in good health. However, two problems, both of the first magnitude, are closing in on the country. First, day in and day out, more people are pensioned out of the work force. This means that there are fewer working people in relation to non-working, that is, children and retirees. Fairly soon the efforts to support the non-workers will demand either higher taxes or lower pensions, or both. There is also a growing demand for a higher retirement age, but the issue is obviously hot, and no leading politician or party has so far dared to take on the problem in earnest. Everybody realizes that the age boom, were the baby boomers will soon play a very prominent role, is a time bomb; so far it's left ticking.

Right now we are at a stage where it is normal to study up to the age of 30. Then comes work, for an ordinary Swede, until he or she is 58, whereupon the person statistically lives another 24 years supported and cared for by the common. In other words: 28 years of work, 54 of preparation and leisure.

Secondly, even if Swedes are extremely healthy by world standards, with age they do get frail, feeble, and sick. The need for nursing and care are on the increase and will go on increasing for the foreseeable future. Again, this means higher taxes or less efficient care. Or, once more: both. It also means that hospitals, nursing homes, and retiree communities will have to be staffed. Since Swedes will not be available, people will have to be imported, mainly from the Middle East and Africa. A large proportion of the newcomers will be Muslims, resulting at best in a soft clash of civilizations, at worst incidents of terrorism and increasing demands for special laws (i.e. Sharia-based) for ever stronger minorities.

To say that Sweden is unprepared for the very dramatic change ahead is understating the problem gravely.

The main difference between immigration in the US and Sweden can be summarized rather quickly:

After the end of the slave trade people have overwhelmingly come to the US, because they wanted to come. They saw a brighter future for themselves and their children in the New World and were prepared to work hard to become part of the American dream.

To Sweden, beginning in the 1970's, people came mainly because they wanted to get away from another country: from war, tyranny, poverty, religious or racial persecution, etc. The immigrant, in other words, was a refugee who sought first and foremost protection.

Not only that.

The US has traditionally been generous with residence and work per-mits, but not particularly generous with benefits guaranteed by the states or the federal government. The authorities have not given newcomers a whole lot of help. But more importantly, much more importantly: they have not stood in the way. There can, of course, be no better proof of this than the fact that there are, as of this writing, some 11-12 million illegal immigrants in the continental US. The borders, particularly the long stretch where the US and Mexico meet, have been (and are) notoriously leaky. Not few of the illegal have been on the wrong side of that border for many years; some 3 million children have been born there and are therefore American citizens. And concurrently with the illegal, a steady stream of legal immigrants have been admitted, according to quotas and rules, but admitted. The newcomers have been given aid and comfort by family members and countrymen, by churches and voluntary organiza-tions, but hardly by the authorities. And once more: they have gotten jobs, the right to work, to get promoted, and to make money.

All this, of course, is not to say that there are not problems. Illegal is, after all, illegal. And the US, as well as Sweden, is changing population fast. As Samuel Huntington reveals in his book Who Are We, in 1960 the largest group of foreign-born people was Italian, 1,257,000; and then came German, 990,000; Canadian, 953,000; British, 833,000; and Polish 748,000.

In the year 2000 the largest foreign-born group is Mexican, 7,841,000; followed by Chinese, 1,391,000; Philippino, 1,288,000; Indian 1,007,000; and Cuban, 952,000.

In other words, the US is very fast being becoming more Latin and more Asian. In the 1990's, Huntington notes, half of all immigrants were Latinos and half of the Latinos were Mexicans.

This situation is unique for the US and unique in the world, Hun-tington writes. No other First World country has a land frontier with a Third World country, much less one of two thousand miles.

Huntington also notes that the Latin immigrants all speak the same language, Spanish, and that the income difference between the US and Mexico is the largest of two adjacent countries in the world.

That the growing Mexicanization of large parts of the US—some talk of a re-conquest—creates massive problems goes without saying. What about social services for illegal immigrants? What about education for their offspring? In which language should children from purely Mexican suburbs or other areas be educated? Since it is physically and perhaps morally impossible to expel 12 million people - it would take an army and several years, tie up courts and administrative offices - how is one going to deal with the problem? Incentives to go home and try to get a visa? Amnesty?

The questions are many and, it must be said, extremely difficult. The US, like Sweden and the other European countries, must ask itself exactly Huntington's question: Who are we? The difference is that in the US the question is really posed, whereas in Europe it is swept under the rug; indeed as I have shown, if you even hint at questions like that, you will be stamped politically incorrect, chauvinist, and racist all in one fell swoop.

If I may venture a guess, and it can be no more than that, the US will be able to solve, or at least live with, its population problems not the least because the population will grow at a healthy rate. And not the least because the old truth about immigrants still holds:

Nobody stopped them. Nobody stood in the way.

That's not the way it worked in Sweden.

To sum up the two countries in three words each, I come up with the following.

The USA:
Freedom.
Work.
Opportunity.
Sweden:
Security.
Equality.
Uniformity.

The New World has always been and still is dynamic and forever changing. The Old World is passive, weary of change and fearful of risk. All of which will be explored further in the next chapter.

Between 2.5 and 7 million Muslims live in the USA. They earn slightly more than the average American. The group is considered well integrated in society.

Some 300,000 Muslims have immigrated to Sweden, mainly from Kurdistan (Turkey, Iran and Iraq), Bosnia and Somalia. Unemployment is high; the groups are not well integrated.

13

Paralysis vs. action

If you want to illustrate the difference between a typical Swede and a typical American you could do worse than to show two pictures. On the left, Ingvar Carlsson, Olof Palme's long time friend and successor. On the right, Ronald Reagan.

The picture of Carlsson shows a seemingly humorless, gray man, cautious to a fault, party insider and politician all his life. Very competent, utterly unflappable, no surprises.

The other picture shows a man, who looks bold, sunny and optimistic and smiles like he had been an actor before he, rather recklessly, went into politics. A high-odds outsider, out of the realm of conventional wisdom (and precisely therefore, much despised by it).

At about the same time Reagan used the expression evil empire (and was hysterically applauded inside the Gulag archipelago, where the inmates knew what evil was), Carlsson claimed that, of course, Communism wasn't all that great, but at least it had solved the material problems of the Soviet Union. A short while later, the Soviet Union collapsed, precisely because it had not solved the problem of feeding and clothing the population, or releasing the creative energies of its people.

Carlsson and most, if not all, Swedish politicians on the left were dead wrong and the ones on the right not much better. They didn't even realize that a country where private people were not allowed to own a typewriter much less a computer could not endure long in the information age. How can you solve problems if you are not allowed to communicate and learn from others? How can you find the best ideas, methods, and products, if no competition is allowed? How on earth can you believe that a bunch of old guys in Moscow can decide, better than the locals can, what is good for Archangelsk or Smolensk?

Yes, it is evident that the leaders of Sweden should have known, but—and never forget this—they didn't. Or, perhaps they knew but for some reason decided that they did not want to take the consequences of that knowledge.

Reagan, on the other hand, was absolutely right. The empire was evil as well as inefficient. The people trapped inside its borders hated it and that's the reason it died.

Swedes like Carlsson saw themselves as smart, well prepared for power, cautious and realistic in the true sense of the word - although they loved to brag about their radicalism. As Swedes are brought up to do, they always searched for the *lagom* solution to all problems—lagom being a word that has no literal translation but means not too much and not too little of everything and, most of all, not too much change. Ironically, Reagan, who called himself conservative, was in the true sense of the word a radical, even revolutionary leader. The Swedes on the other hand wanted to preserve status quo at almost any cost, not the least because it preserved their own power.

Reagan—the quintessential American—in spite of grave risk, decided to set out to change the world.

Which he did.

As a far better observer than I, the *New York Times* columnist, James Reston wrote in his in inimitable way:

"After chasing politicians for forty years, I thought I was beyond surprise, but I didn't count on Ronald Reagan. He made more friends, had more fun, fooled more people, presided over more sustained prosperity, incurred more debt, controlled more nuclear missiles, encouraged more individual freedom at home and abroad, and escaped responsibility for more scandals than any president in the history of the Republic and was more popular at the end of two terms in the White House than he was at the beginning. Of all the fantastic success films produced by Hollywood, few, if any, compared with Ronald Reagan's own true story of the poor boy from Illinois, who was twice elected president of the United States…"

Reston also wrote that the Americans probably liked Reagan so much because they felt like he was like them: optimistic, ready to take chances and determined to do great things with and for the country.

It must be added, of course, that a small and powerless country, close to a cruel and inhuman giant, must play its cards, in so far that it has any cards to play, with great caution. It would, of course, have been ridiculous for Carlsson (or, in his days, Palme) to go to the Berlin Wall and shout, "Mr. Gorbachev, tear down this wall!" Neither would it have been wise to cry out for regime change in Eastern Europe. If Carlsson had tried to copy Reagan he would have been mad (and also definitely not elected).

That much is clear. But why did Carlsson have to make excuses for Communism? And why did Sweden have to brand Reagan a trigger-happy cowboy, a dunce, and a B-film actor? Why was Afghanistan never condemned the way Vietnam was? Why were Israelis always the bad boys and the corrupt and dictatorial Arafat a hero?

Part of the answer is that caution, like power, corrupts. It becomes a part of the system, a tool, indeed a weapon to use against each and everyone who demands change—in reality, against change itself. Don't rock the boat. Steady as you go, and tag even the most innocuous proposal for change as sheer adventurism. If evidence is needed look again at a basic fact:

The same party has ruled Sweden since 1932 (the year before the author of this book was born), with two pitiful interruptions. After the Second World War, Sweden has had non-socialist governments only 15 percent of the time; Norway follows with 33 and Denmark with 42. You have to go to Mexico or Japan to find a democratic one party state like Sweden.

Not only that. During the two periods the non-socialists did in fact govern, they did their utmost to copy the policies they had pretended to be against. Indeed, the non-socialists in the 1970's socialized more of the Swedish industry than the Social Democrats ever did, albeit because the oil crisis had them cornered and their experience in government was extremely limited.

In the same period the US has had 12 presidents—six Democrats and six Republican—or, in other words: regular change, including not only the top spots but large parts of the administration. It should also be noted that the difference between presidents out of the same party, say Eisenhower and Reagan or Truman and Clinton, can be considerable, while Swedish politicians often seem interchangeable, regardless of age, gender, or party. Perhaps Gunnar Strömmer, chairman of the conservative party's youth organization, expressed the Swedish political system best, when, after the 1998 election, he explained that it was a competition between seven Social democratic parties...

In the campaign of 1980, Ronald Reagan said:

"Our optimism has once more been turned loose. And all of us recognize that these people who keep talking about the age of limits are really talking about their own limitation, not America's."

Jimmy Carter was, at least openly, more religious than Reagan. He went to church, read the Bible and so on, but the Southern Evangelicals chose to desert him just the same. It was the secular American religion, optimism, which did him in. Carter was humiliated when the Iranians took all the diplomats and other embassy workers in Tehran as hostages and an attempt to free them failed badly. The second oil crisis and the long gas lines hit his popularity hard. But most of all, he brought himself down. According to many well-qualified observers he might have been one of the most intelligent presidents ever. He was a formidable manager of the White House (including the tennis courts) but with common Americans, he simply didn't connect. In the famous philosopher Isaiah Berlin's classification of politicians, he was a fox, who knew many little things; Reagan was the porcupine who knew one big thing - that thing being that America has not only to be number one, but also to feel that it is number one. Which, not incidentally, also meant that the Evil Empire must be defeated. No longer contained, no longer feared and coddled by some, but defeated.

Swedish politicians regularly denounced the balance of terror, which saved the world from a nuclear holocaust. Little did they understand that they, the hardnosed realists had actually fallen in love with the stalemate. They could play (or thought they could play) the superpowers against each other. They could condemn the over-reliance on armies and weapons, but it took Reagan to come up with Star Wars and challenge the whole concept of MAD (Mutual Assured Destruction) and by doing so created a whole new reality.

Quite naturally, in Sweden only people considered more or less hopelessly conservative (a highly negative word), reactionary (worse), or neo liberal (about as bad as neo con), gave Reagan any credit for the fall of the Evil Empire. Well, he might have helped a little bit in shoving them into the abyss, but in reality the system collapsed all by itself. It had not, you see, been truly socialistic, like it was supposed to be in the days of Lenin; it degenerated into dictatorship under Stalin and never reformed. The thing that made the people put up with all these evil commissars in the Kremlin was the pressure from the US and NATO. Had the West been, like Sweden, more understanding, more softly accommodating, the collapse would have come much earlier.

With this as background, it should surprise nobody that the Swedes were mildly positive during Bill Clinton's eight years in the Oval Office. Democrats are always more popular in Sweden, mainly for the reason that they are considered closer to the people, particularly those who are poor or black or both. In Sweden it is considered a fact written in stone that a large part of the American population is destitute. This is true to an extent, but what the Swedes don't know (and media definitely does not report) is that the poor are not the same people year after year. As several surveys show, there is a constant flow of people from low-paying jobs to better ones. And besides, to be poor in a very rich country like the States, is not the same thing as being poor in a poor country. Indeed many statistically poor Americans would not change places with Swedes living on the dole. Though by gaining financial security, they would subsist on a very low level with no chance of bettering their lot. So, life in the US is indeed riskier; you are free to succeed but also to fail - while life in Sweden offers more security but also less opportunity; I'll explain this more in detail a little further on in this chapter.

If the Swedes liked Clinton, albeit in a lukewarm way, they detest his successor. As earlier stated, no American president has come so close to being actually hated as George W. Bush. Reagan might have been a little dense, but after all, he had charm and he did negotiate with that nice Russian, Gorbachev, didn't he? But Bush!

Well, there was a wave of sympathy and solidarity after 9-11. Nobody really objected very much to the war against the Taliban in Afghanistan, maybe because nobody cared much about a country so far away; Sweden even sent a few soldiers to help with peacekeeping when the hostilities ended.

With Iraq, it was different. Sweden, which holds the United Nations in almost religious awe, could not condone that the US attacked without a green light from the Security Council. With a few notable exceptions, nobody loved Saddam Hussein, but the political establishment from left to right fervently believed that small nations must band together and stop the bigger ones from acting unilaterally even to stop a murderous dictator from making life hellish for 25 million people. Again, one saw only danger in change, no opportunity, only danger. The fact that many Americans saw the war the same way enforced the belief that W was a madman for many Swedes, the fact that the President is a born again Christian is proof enough. Many Swedes were clearly happy that the war went badly and almost nobody agreed that fundamentalist Islam constituted a threat to Europe, including Sweden, as well as to America and Israel. In police and media circles it became known that there were terrorist cells in Stockholm as well as London, Berlin, and other cities. But we, the Swedes mainly shrugged. "So what," said the proverbial man in the street; trains and subways might be blown up in Madrid and London, plans to murder thousands of air line passengers might be revealed, but, well, it won't happen here.

Swedes, in short, looked upon themselves as immune against terror and bombs, as inside the world and yet at the same time safely outside.

Looking at the structure of the country, this attitude is hardly surprising.

As far as foreign policy is concerned, it soon became clear that if a young diplomat wanted to advance and be given a position at one of the big and coveted embassies in Washington, London, Paris, Brussels or (if you were close to retirement) Rome, Oslo, Copenhagen, or Helsinki, you had better have the politically correct opinions. As ambassador Jan Mårtensson put it in his memoirs:

"One saw the light in the tunnel and deserted the true faith for an even truer. *Svenska Dagbladet* (conservative) was exchanged for *Arbetet* (Social Democratic), radical opinions were banded about in the cafeteria and as eagerly as visibly and laudably one shared the opinions of those in power."

But this was not only at the foreign office— far from it. During the last years of the 20th century the Social Democrats placed their men or women in almost all key positions throughout the administration. At the turn of the century, the majority of bishops, generals, directors general, university professors, and ambassadors were Social Democrats or sympathizers. The same is true for the leaders of schools, museums, and theaters, not to speak of social services centers, hospitals, and nursery schools, meaning, of course, that books and other material used in education were chosen to please those (almost) always in power.

To get a place in the sun, you better conform. To give but one example, once again consider Anitra Steen, who has been director general of the Swedish counterpart of the IRS, director general of the authority that supervises the universities, State Secretary (which means number 2) in the Finance Ministry, and, nowadays CEO of the state liquor monopoly. In all these positions, she has worked closely together with Prime Minister Göran Persson, whom she recently married. Other close friends of the PM have been promoted to equally elevated positions. Charges of nepotism have been aired in the media by, among others, Inga-Britt Ahlenius, today in a high position at the UN. The charges were met with a shrug. Indeed nobody seriously questioned Ms. Steen's competence for two positions so widely different as chief of the tax services and head of liquor sales.

The courts are, of course, supposed to be independent in each and every way, but the most important judge-ships and other jobs regularly go to jurists with good connections, meaning that they know and appeal to the right people in the judicial system. This particular form of cross-fertilization of course, influences the new laws as well as the application of older laws.

Since authors, painters, and other artists are quite often dependent on subsidies from the state or municipalities, it pays for intellectuals to conform. Media people conform a little bit less maybe, but criticize mainly details, though hardly ever the underlying ideology. Only one leading columnist, *Dagens Nyheter*'s Hans Bergström, was bold enough to claim that Sweden has become a one party state. (He said it not in the important newspaper but in an interview in a very small magazine, but at least he said it.)

The above says a lot. But we need to go further. The bureaucracy infiltrates almost every nook and cranny of Swedish life. We have bureaucrats who are supposed to help people get jobs, energy counselors, environmental advisers, cultural secretaries, youth consultants, hospital administrators, psychologists, and hospital workers, people who have to see to it that there is no racial discrimination, people who have to see to it that there is no discrimination against women, people who have to see to it that there is no discrimination against homosexuals, and so on and on and on. We should also mention the fact that many municipalities have not only the political leaders but also a whole host of experts in various fields on their payrolls. All these people have a vested interest in keeping the system just the way it is, preferably adding a service here or a couple of bureaucrats there, but first and foremost, to resist change in any way. If the Swedish system would have another name, it would certainly be: NO CHANGE.

A natural consequence of the Social Democratic hegemony is that sports associations, farmers cooperatives, doctors associations, and many, many other non-governmental organizations with a lot of power and influence tend to pick leaders who either belong to the Social Democratic party, sympathize with it, or at the very least, know how to behave well enough to get financial assistance.

The biggest non-governmental organization is the LO, the giant trade union conglomerate that organizes practically all blue collar and other workers in the country. LO bosses like Arne Geijer, Gunnar Nilsson,

Stig Malm and today's chairwoman, Wanja Lundby-Wedin are regularly said to be more powerful than whoever is Prime Minister. Without enormous financial contributions from LO and the work of thousands of functionaries it would be very difficult indeed for the Social Democrats to win elections.

The aid, of course, comes with a price tag. To get it, the government must make laws that are labor friendly.

As I noted in chapter 10 about the 1970's, the most labor friendly of all laws makes it almost impossible to fire anybody... which in turn means that an employer must be extremely cautious when it comes to hiring somebody. A Swede, like a Japanese, has come to expect that the first job he or she gets will be his or hers for life.

Or at least until the age of 65. And regardless of whether it feels good or not.

Again: no change...

Another keyword is dependence. It is easily explained:

What does an institution for the treatments of alcoholism need most of all? Right - alcoholics.

What happens if there are not enough alcoholics? Well, the institution will go out of business.

Writing this I'm not implying any devilish conspiracy. I do not think that Swedish doctors and counselors wish their patients, be they alcoholics or diabetics, to remain sick. On the other hand, if there are many clients around the various agencies, not the least the ones dealing with people incapacitated to work, they will flower and expand while many needy people flock to their doors. So, why not prolong a sick leave (paid with tax money)? Why not design a long and complicated treatment? Why not, yes, indeed why not invent new afflictions needing treatment, new groups of people to be drawn into the system?

Without sick people, no doctors...

Without a plethora of subsidies, there is no need for an army of bureaucrats to administer the subsidies. Without a lot of activities, there is no need to expand the agency (and propel its bosses into higher positions). Friends need jobs. Party members need encouragement, for instance by being offered positions in the giant state and municipal machinery.

Never Enough, Always More is the title of one of the few books that tried to describe the system. A power machine, I myself wrote in an earlier book.

Since then the system of interdependence has only grown. "Have we passed the point of no return?" internationally renowned political economist Assar Lundbeck asked towards the end of the 1990's.

I think the answer is yes. And no return can only mean one thing: paralysis.

The USA has 313 billionaires in US dollars. Richest is Microsoft founder, Bill Gates with $48 billion, followed by the "Sage of Omaha" investment specialist Warren Buffet, $41 billion, and Microsoft co-founder Paul Allen, $20 billion. In the USA there are 8.9 million millionaires, i.e. men or women with a net worth of 1 million or more, excluding a prime residence.

Sweden has 9 billionaires in US dollars. Leading the list is Ingvar Kamprad, founder of furniture chain Ikea, with assets of $23 billion. He is followed by Stefan Persson, owner of clothing chain Hennes & Mauritz, with $11.2 billion, and Hans Rausing of Tetra Pak Packaging group with $8.2 billion.

48,500 Swedes have a million dollars or more in net holdings, exclusive of prime residence.

The richest Americans all reside in the US. Of the Swedes, Kamprad lives in Switzerland, Rausing in the UK.

14

Where do we stand today?

As this is being written at the beginning of 2007, there is no denying that the US is the strongest power on Earth, ever. Stronger than Rome or the British Empire, stronger than China or the once giant Soviet Union ever were.

The US is, together with Russia, the only power that can literally destroy civilization, as we know it, a situation that has existed since the 1960's. It is alone in being able to project military power in every corner of the world and soon enough in many areas of space. Helped by a military machine of unprecedented force it has built up influence and presence not only in Europe and East Asia (as a result of World War II) but also in Central Asia, Afghanistan, the Middle East, Africa, and to some extent India. It has military strong points all around the globe but occupation forces only in Iraq; unlike the empires of old it does not wish to possess colonies.

It must be stressed that the US military superiority will actually grow for decades to come; when and if China achieves some kind of parity is still unclear; that Europe should even try is unlikely.

The new American Empire is, as this book has hopefully shown, an empire not only of military might and political influence, but even more so of commerce and innovation, of communications and life styles. To say that people all over the world wear jeans and drink Coke is a truism; all around, young and old use Google and MSWord; American TV shows and Hollywood movies dominate from Jordan to Tahiti to Tromsö, and news is more or less synonymous with CNN, Fox, or CNBC. Indeed more and more European reporting of events in Africa or Asia builds on second hand American sources. With market forces being what they are, this dependence will increase (in spite of intensive criticism in intellectual circles, there simply is no alternative). To a large extent

Americans decide (luckily in many different ways, in my opinion) what the world is going to know about the world. More Americans win Nobel prizes than the citizens of other countries—the fact that many of these successful scientists came to the US quite recently from countries in Europe or Asia, of course, doesn't change anything in that regard. Nothing breeds like success and the US remains—and will remain—the great magnet for talented people, mainly because the resources and rewards it offers are incomparable. Because of the global phenomenon known as outsourcing, more and more Americanized enclaves develop in far away countries—witness, to give but one example, the IT boom in the Indian city of Bangalore. That the top talent of the enclaves is drawn to centers like Silicon Valley, Massachusetts, or Austin, Texas, is a certainty, just as it is a certainty that the top US universities will (in spite of the aftermath of 9-11) continue to attract a fair share of the best and the brightest students from all corners of the world.

More importantly, much more, is the fact that the US will remain everybody's second homeland. Ordinary people will continue to cross the Atlantic or the Mexican border with the intention of working hard and being a part of the American dream. Many will fail, but more will succeed and immigration will guarantee steady expansion and a steady supply of new ideas.

In short: after World War I finished off Europe as the world power, via World War II and the Cold War, the future for the US has become ever brighter. Its strength in military, economic, scientific, and cultural matters is unequalled; its energy and creativity are without comparison.

In the context of a book such as this one, it is of the highest importance to stress that the increase in influence for the US as a player in world politics has been matched by a steady increase in standard of living for ordinary, American citizens. As told in various other chapters in the book, as far as GDP per capita is concerned—that is, very roughly, personal, disposable income after tax—the US stands supreme. On the average, Americans live in homes almost twice as big as average Swedish homes. There are some 800 TV sets for 1,000 citizens, as compared to 500 for that many Swedes. Of the countries of Europe, only little Luxemburg (a tax haven) is as rich as the richest American states; Sweden would rank among the poorest, say Alabama and Oklahoma.

Only when it comes to cell phones is Sweden clearly ahead. Around the turn of the century every fourth Swede had a cell phone, against every fiftieth in the US. The difference, however, is fast disappearing; Steve Jobs' incredible new iPhone may be the beginning of a faster pace in making people mobile.

Of course there are dangers ahead, but how important are they? Let's discuss them briefly, one by one.

THE WAR ON TERRORISM. No, it cannot be won in the way a conventional war can be won. The Muslim countries, Pakistan and Indonesia, as well as the Arab states will continue to produce terrorists. Suicide bombers will probably appear in cities on the US mainland; embassies and individual citizens will be attacked. There will, inevitably, be casualties.

The possibility that the casualties will sometimes be considerable - that the attacks will truly hurt - should not be underestimated. Terrorists, financed by oil money (and thus, by American gas guzzlers!) might get their hands on a dirty, nuclear bomb or even a regular warhead. A detonation in New York or Washington or LA will create enormous pain and suffering and no doubt panic. So will a dirty nuclear bomb. But, and this is the important thing, it cannot happen often. It can destroy or seriously damage a great city, but it does not threaten the existence of the US. In other words: the terrorists cannot win in the classical sense and chances are relatively good that truly horrible acts (like the ones described) can be prevented. As for the risk that the US will develop into a rigid and dehumanized police state, I am not worried; the civil society is extremely strong and abuse of human rights simply will not be tolerated. And there is always the hope that in time the Muslim world will become more democratic, less fanatical, and less likely to produce terrorists.

On the other hand, it would be foolish to believe that the road to peace will be easy. The world is full of conflicts. Groups and individuals that feel wronged will take up arms and attack people who, they feel, are guilty of oppressing or exploiting them or sometimes because they believe in different gods. The US will almost always be involved because the world community demands that the US takes it upon itself to end the conflict before it becomes too violent or wide spread. The simple fact is that no one else has the ability.

In other words: troubles there will be. And expense of lives and treasures. The US will be much admired and even more maligned.

A country such as Sweden, small and situated in a very peaceful corner of the earth, will, on the whole, play quite insignificant roles in the new great game, much to the chagrin of politicians and intellectuals who will forever say (and believe) that they could have handled the so-called situations much, much better.

ROGUE STATES. Yes, states like Iran and North Korea will present a challenge. As far as North Korea is concerned, almost anything could happen at just about any time. It could attack South Korea or Japan (but not yet the US) with nuclear weapons and a strong, conventional army. It would be defeated (and perhaps annihilated) but the whole world would suffer from radioactive contamination as well as an inevitable economic depression.

Iran most likely will not have atomic weapons in another eight to ten years, counting from 2006. Maybe, just maybe, the ongoing negotiations can stop the enrichment process and establish international control, but this does not seem very likely. Therefore, the most probable scenario is that Iran will one day have the Bomb. If the fundamentalist followers of Ayatollah Khomeini that have run the country since 1979 are still in power, three possibilities must be considered:

1.   Tehran makes good on its threat and tries to destroy Israel. The Israelis retaliate. Both countries suffer unheard of damage; Israel, because of its tiny surface, is mortally wounded.

2.   Israel mounts a preventive attack, most likely with the support of the US, overt or tacit. There is a fair chance that Iran is disarmed, but no certainty exists. A long war and a violent upsurge in Muslim terrorism are inevitable.

3.   A balance of terror, modeled on the Cold War, or the situation prevailing between India and Pakistan since 1998, is established. The passing of time and the development of trade, and maybe cultural exchange and tourism may ease the stalemate. There is a chance that the regime in Tehran will soften or even be overthrown. Another possibility is a drawn-out conflict of the so called asymmetric kind: steadily better-armed groups like Hizbollah or Hamas chipping away at Israeli and American interests, provoking sometimes violent reactions and much turmoil in domestic politics.

All in all, the best hope for a peaceful solution is negotiations, in which the US must take part together with the EU, and more importantly, Russia and China, who both have the possibility to hinder an agreement. The carrots offered to Iran in the form of trade, technological aid, and more influence in international affairs must be carefully counterbalanced with the threat of force. In other words, the US must let it be clearly known that its patience is not unlimited and that it carries a big stick. In time Russia, which lives in a demographic nightmare, losing perhaps a million citizens per year, will play a bigger role in helping contain Iran, a country the leaders in the Kremlin will clearly not want to see too powerful.

IRAQ. It's easy to say that the operation in Iraq must succeed. It's considerably harder to state what success means. Is a weak, divided, and now and then chaotic democracy enough? Would it be better if a reasonably benign dictator - no Saddam, of course - appeared and stabilized the situation? What should the US do if there is a big and messy civil war between the three main ethnic groups? Isolate the Kurds, maybe, by granting them support for statehood (and getting on bad terms with Turkey, Iran, and various others)? Try to make peace between Shias and Sunnis? By diplomacy? By force? Alone? With allies? Or, should the US maybe retreat, keep a keen eye on other countries in the neighborhood (particularly oil giant Saudi Arabia) and let the conflict consummate itself? How is one then to stop Iran, where the majority of the population is Shia, from gaining dominance over Iraq where Shiites, once brutally persecuted under Saddam, today have control over the government? To these and other similar questions, there are no certain answers. Except that the ball will be in the US court, because in my opinion and in the foreseeable future, it always will be. US policy has perhaps not failed (although it might be on its way) but neither has it succeeded, and it is absolutely certain that the president elected in 2008 will have just as many problems with the rest of the world as George W. Bush, who, by *New York Times* columnist Thomas Friedman, was labeled the most hated president in history. To be precise, there is no way the US can rectify all wrongs (or even most of them) or eliminate each and every crisis. It will always be criticized for doing too little or doing too much, for being too timid and too slow or for being too aggressive. It will be lonesome at the top, but is there an alternative? I think not.

OIL. The US is consuming around 20 percent of all oil produced in the world, some 21 million barrels per day, considerably more than Western Europe (with a much larger population) and so far, more than China, Japan and India combined. But resources are not unlimited, and as competition becomes more and more fierce it is quite clear that something will have to give if outright war about oil is going to be avoided. This means that the US as well as other industrialized and industrializing countries must find energy sources other than petroleum or natural gas to drive factories, heat homes, and run cars. As of now, no nation, with the possible exception of France, has anything like a coherent energy policy. A first step in the US could be to raise gasoline taxes to a more realistic level, meaning $3.50 per gallon gasoline at the pump, and to invest in nuclear energy, ethanol, and renewable energy sources. Other nations must be encouraged to do the same, most particularly China and India, whose future needs are no doubt the greatest, but also Western Europe and others. That the world outside the Middle East, mostly the US, goes on financing dictatorships and terrorists because of its unquenchable thirst for oil is, to put it mildly, not a viable option.

ENVIRONMENT. Again, the state that produces almost 25 percent of the world's BNP and a similar amount of the pollution and environmental degradation that goes with it, must take the lead. This obviously means not only enforcing good environmental standards at home, but also taking the lead in working out international agreements and convincing governments (notably the one in Beijing) that unchecked industrial expansion simply is not sustainable. Or to put it in more realistic and therefore starker terms: it will lead to consequences too catastrophic to contemplate. Time is not on anybody's side and only the US has sufficient scientific, financial, and political resources to lead the fight for a livable world. That private enterprise, like carmakers and oil companies, will play a leading role is self-evident. There is no power like the power of the market, and as this book is being written more and more signs point in the right direction.

POWER. The disarmers have it wrong. It is of the utmost importance, for the US itself and for the democratic world, and indeed the not so democratic part as well, that the US remains the pre-eminent power. In a number of years, maybe before 2020 or 25, it will certainly be challenged by China, armed and dangerous (if it has not, by that time, imploded, which is also a possibility). To remain superior and therefore able to establish a new balance of terror, maybe less aggressive, but in no way less necessary than the old one, the US must go on constructing a missile defense (even for Europe) and fielding offensive forces ready to engage anywhere in the world to prevent war or unrest to spread. NATO must be induced to take care of a range of situations even outside the European homeland. An eventual membership for Russia should not be ruled out.

However one looks at it, the US president will, in the foreseeable future be the most powerful man or woman on Planet Earth. No other human being is going to have greater responsibility for the defense of democracy and civilization. Therefore the means to take on any comer simply must be at hand even if it is always going to be preferable to solve conflicts with peaceful means.

FINANCES. The Federal Government of the United States is in debt. So are the majority of American families.

First, the government. When the clock on Times Square in New York started to show the size of the Federal Debt in 1989 it was 2.7 trillion dollars. In the second quarter of 2006 it had grown to 8.3 trillion or 3.8 percent of GDP. At the same time the currency deficit (mainly through trade) is growing. The difference between assets owned by Americans abroad and what foreigners own in the US is 20 percent in favor of the foreigners. The biggest lender of all is China, who in 2005 purchased US Treasury Bonds valued at some 2 percent of GDP, a truly dramatic sum made even more remarkable by the fact that it means that Chinese, who make an average $1,500 per year, are lending money to Americans making $40,000 a year. Other big creditors are Japan and the oil producing countries in the Middle East.

At the same time, individual American citizens are deeply in debt. Combined savings are less than 0 and sinking. Social Security, Medicare, and Medicaid consume nearly half of the federal government's revenues and will grow ever more expensive as the graying of the population continues.

Which all means that though decisions and quite a lot of belt tightening lies ahead, the whole world is dependent on the US economy staying the course. Several percentages of the world's combined work forces in fact work for US consumers. If Mr. and Mrs. Jones stop buying, worldwide unemployment will rise in a truly frightening way.

That Sweden finds itself in a very different position is saying the obvious, and not only because of the difference in size and power between the two countries.

While the US can rely on both a relatively high birth rate and a steady influx of young, work-hungry and often talented people from all parts of the globe, Swedish women do not bear enough babies for the population to grow (statistically the birth rate is 1.85 or less per woman and thus under the reproduction rate of 2.1). Expansion can be achieved only by immigration, which, as chapter 12 shows, brings with it many problems. To these problems, I will return, but first a few words to describe the state of the Kingdom at the beginning of the third millennium.

DEFENSE. It is not needed anymore in the traditional sense of the word and quite rightly it has been almost abolished. There is no longer any risk of an attack by the Soviet Union. All of the neighbors are friendly, and all except Norway are members of the European Union, meaning that war is in fact impossible. Sweden still has a fairly large air force, mainly to keep Saab's factories going, making the trade unions happy and the Wallenberg group a bit richer. That the air force itself has so little money that many of the planes are never flown, is a bit of a scandal, which will disappear when the current generation of fighter bombers is phased out without replacements being ordered. As far as ground forces are concerned, they are trimmed, trimmed, and trimmed, and made professional in so far that a few quite good units are ready to take part in international peacekeeping (like in Afghanistan, but not, of course, Iraq). Neither the defense forces, nor the police, have any good idea of how to defend the country's four nuclear power plants against terrorist attacks—a nightmare for many of us, but evidently not for the leaders of the country. Another problem is the high cost of the defense - or rather non-defense. It has so far turned out to be just as expensive to demobilize the forces as to maintain them. A special consideration is, as always in Sweden, the risk that the decommissioning of forces and closing of bases will make for greater unemployment. Sweden is *not* the US and the tendency is strong to look at just about any job as guaranteed employment for life.

FOREIGN POLICY. It is tempting to say that a foreign policy no longer exists, and in a way such a claim would be true. As a member of the EU, Sweden, as well as all other members must abide by decisions taken in Brussels. These decisions are not taken, as all too many people believe, by the European Commission or the European Parliament, but by representatives of the 25 governments, meaning endless discussions, compromises, and enormous chances of hiding behind the backs of others. In other words, when a decision is not popular at home, a Swedish minister can always blame Brussels and the bureaucrats. If, on the other hand, the decision is popular, he can just as easily claim that he himself was really one of the main authors of that particular reform. The reality of the matter is, of course, that the bigger states, in particular Germany and France and sometimes Britain and Italy make the decisions much more often than Denmark or Sweden. When it comes to life or death questions, like nuclear arms for Iran, the three big ones take it upon themselves to negotiate for the EU, with the foreign minister of the organization, Xavier Solana, as more or less an onlooker. Sweden's input is negligible. The same goes for farm policy (scandalously dictated by France) and a host of other issues.

It should be noted that the Swedish voters said no to membership in the European Monetary Union (EMU) and did not adopt the common currency, the Euro. It is generally seen as a lukewarm union member; to say that the common Swede is a great enthusiast for Europe would be a grave exaggeration. Yet, it should be noted that there is a strong belief among common folks that Sweden is listened to and among the leading members, maybe because of a mystic, particular wisdom. That politicians like people to believe this goes without saying while, in fact, globalization and swifter communications have made small countries less and less influential.

ECONOMY. As already told, Sweden is and has always been totally dependent on world markets. It became global for keeps long before almost every other country did and certainly before the US. As told before, it has become more dependent on exporting from platforms in other countries, meaning that it has become more and more difficult to keep decision making in Sweden. For instance, the styling and technical make- up of Volvo cars is still decided in Gothenburg, but must be cleared with Ford's headquarters in Michigan, which obviously has the last word. The same goes for Saab, owned by GM and long plagued by quality problems and losses, to the extent that its Swedish factories might one day be closed down. Since the 1960's, Sweden has lost roughly 100,000 industrial jobs each decade, how many due to increased efficiency and how many due to globalization is not well known.

SOCIAL STRUCTURE. As already shown, Sweden in 2006 had almost 25 percent of the working age population out of work. Add to that the retired people, more than 2 million and growing, and the 1,352,000 employed by the government and the municipalities, and you find that the income of more than half the population is paid by tax money. Since many people working for private enterprises are also dependent on various kinds of subsidies, the dependence on the state and the municipalities is even higher, and very many Swedes, perhaps a majority (there are no certain statistics) could be categorized as working poor.

As I note in Chapter 12, a disproportionate number of the unemployed are so called new Swedes, who came to Sweden not necessarily to find work, but to escape wars, unrest, or poverty. These new Swedes (also called foreigners) live in segregated suburbs, mainly around the three largest cities, Stockholm, Gothenburg, and Malmö. While one could perhaps not speak of them as slums in a classic sense, places like Rinkeby, Tensta, Flemmingsberg and Husby in Stockholm, Bergsjön in Gothenburg and, most particularly, Rosengård in Malmö suffer from unemployment, alienation, and crime. In all these suburbs, you see TV antennas directed towards the old home country; many of the inhabitants speak little or no Swedish; there has been neither integration nor assimilation.

CRIME. There is today more crime in Sweden than in New York City, with a comparable population. In recent years violent crime has gone up sharply, worst of all rape; indeed the statistics indicate that Sweden is suffering a rape epidemic. Some 10 cases are reported to the police every day, but, as everyone knows, many rape victims for various reasons do not care to go to the police, and according to some experts only one rape in five is reported. Since only one out of every five reported cases is brought to court, it is quite clear that the problem is critical, so much more so as there is no doubt that young Muslim men commit rape much more often than Swedes of the old kind—in other words, Swedes born to ethnically Swedish parents. Indeed, as mentioned earlier in the book, there are indications that many gangs of new Swedes see rape of Swedish girls as an act of war against a society they have come to despise because of its arrogance and discrimination (real or perceived). Out of political correctness, which is very strong in Sweden, both media and authorities avoid discussing the rape phenomenon in ethnic terms; official statistics are not permitted to note nationality or origin of offenders.

Sweden's gravest problem in the new century is without doubt demography. The US is bound to grow; Sweden is condemned to shrink, or at least change its population entirely!

As already noted Swedish couples do not have enough babies to keep the population constant, much less increase it. The same goes for most of Europe. Russia, the hardest hit nation loses around a million souls a year, mainly to alcohol, TBC, and hepatitis. A little further down the road, when more AIDS cases die, the population explosion will worsen and, in fifty years or so, Russia will be much smaller than its neighbor Iran (see above). At that time, Germany's population too will have shrunk to half its present size, that is, if there is no immigration.

Sweden, because of its high immigration, loses people more slowly than Russia or Germany (or Italy or Spain). Instead it changes population. If present trends hold, in five years, a couple of cities the size of Ronneby or Kristianstad will have changed from old Swedish, to new Swedish—in other words, from places were families have lived for maybe hundreds of years to places where everyone has recently arrived, almost certainly without knowing the language and probably without skills applicable in the labor market.

Mainly Muslims will almost certainly populate the virtually new cities that are created by immigration. As stated in Chapter 13, there are already some 400,000 Muslim believers in in Sweden, almost 4.5 percent of the population. This means that Islam is by far the fastest growing religion in a country where Christendom has long been in rapid decline.

Will this lead to a Christian awakening? To religious conflicts? To conversion of ordinary Swedes to Islam?

The answer still is too early to tell, but the drama deepens when you take age into the picture. Again, all of Europe is graying and Sweden is not bucking the trend. Today there are 5,180,000 people of working age in the country; in 2030 there will be only 4,990,000, which means that ever fewer will have to support a growing number of elderly dependents. Given the fact that people live longer and longer lives (a trend unbroken in Western countries since small pox was brought under control), the burden will become heavier and heavier. Which leads to the conclusion that an elderly Swede, such as myself, will not unlikely spend his last years in a hospital or nursing home, tended to by immigrants from Somalia or Iran, who might, or might not, speak the old man's language.

All in all, when my story ends, Sweden has through the centuries gone from great power to pre-eminent welfare state and industrial powerhouse, to multicultural experiment conducted on the outskirts of Europe, dependent on import of young people from Muslim countries, wholly without influence in world affairs and economically and financially marginalized.

End of story.

According to the CIA report about the world in 2020, the USA will still be the leading country, but weaker in relation to China and India, who have achieved eminence in certain technological and scientific sectors. Big corporations dominate development more and more regardless of state. Many of these companies will have their headquarters in China, India or Brazil, but most will be American.

According to other sources, most big Swedish companies will by that time be dominated by foreign capital.

The US Military Forces employ 1,426,713 men and women on active duty. The defence budget approaches $600 billion and is larger than the budgets of all other countries combined. American men and women are based in more than 700 bases in 36 countries (in the year 2005). The largest contingents are found in Iraq (160,000) and Germany (64,000). The US has around 6,000 + military air crafts and thousands of nuclear and thermonuclear warheads.

Sweden's defence budget is SEK 40 million, a figure that surprises many observers since it has remained the same in spite of the fact that Sweden has disarmed at a fairly rapid rate since the collapse of the Soviet Union in 1991. Sweden has just over 200 JAS Gripen fighter bombers on duty (although most of them are mothballed). The Swedish army consists of 8,000 men and a few women. The law says that every young man can be conscripted into the defense forces; however only around a fifth get to serve. During the Second World War, as well as the Cold War, the doctrine was that the whole country (450,000 sq km) should be defended. At times more than 500,000 men were in uniform at the same time. Now the soldiers are trained mainly to be able to do duty on UN-accepted peace missions, such as the one in Afghanistan.

Swedish Kings beginning with Gustaf Vasa

[Trying to make sense of how the different Kings got their names and were numbered is no easy task. There's really no logic to this, so don't even try. ed.]

The Vasa Dynasty / Vasaätten

Gustav Vasa	1521 (1523) – 1560
Erik XIV	1560 – 1568
Johan III	1568 – 1592
Sigismund	1592 – 1599
Karl IX	1599 – 1611
Gustav II Adolf	1611-1632
Regency / Förmyndarstyre	1632 – 1644
Kristina	1644 – 1654

The Pfalz Dynasty / Pfalziska ätten

Karl X Gustav	1654 – 1660
Regency / Förmyndarstyre	1660 – 1672
Karl XI	1672 – 1697
Karl XII	1697 – 1718
Ulrika Eleonora	1719 – 1720

The Hessish Dynasty / Hessiska ätten

Fredrik I	1720 – 1751

The Holstein-Gottorp Dynasty / Holstein-Gottorpska ätten

Adolf Fredrik	1751 – 1771
Gustav III	1771 – 1792
Regency / Förmyndarstyre	1792 – 1796
Gustav IV Adolf	1796 – 1809
Karl XIII	1809 – 1818

The Bernadotte Dynasty / Bernadotteska ätten

Karl XIV Johan	1818 – 1844
Oscar I	1844 – 1859
Karl XV	1859 – 1872
Oscar II	1872 – 1907
Gustav V	1907 – 1950
Gustav VI Adolf	1950 – 1973
Karl XVI Gustaf	1973 –

Prime Ministers in Sweden after WWI

1917 – 1920	Nils Edén (Social Democrats, liberals in a coalition)
1920	Hjalmar Branting (Social Democarats)
1920 – 1921	Louis de Geer (expeditionsministär)
1921	Oscar von Sydow (ditto – intermediate)
1921 – 1923	Hjalmar Branting (Social Democarats)
1923 – 1924	Ernst Trygger (Conservatives—"Högern")
1924 – 1925	Hjalmar Branting (Social Democarats)
1925 – 1926	Rickard Sandler (Social Democarats)
1926 – 1928	Carl Gustaf Ekman (Liberals—Frisinnade Folkpartier, liberala riksdagspartiet)
1928 – 1930	Aevid Lindman (Högern)
1930 – 1932	Carl Gustaf Ekman (Liberals—Frisinnade Folkpartier)
1932	Felix Hamrin (Liberals—Frisinnade Folkpartiet)
1932 – 1936	Per Albin Hansson (Social Democrats)
1936	Axel Persson-Bramstorp (Liberal Farmers' party—Bondeförbundet)
1936 – 1939	Per Albin Hansson (Social Democrats and the Bondeförbundet)
1939 – 1945	Per Albin Hansson (Coalition of all parties)
1945 – 1946	Per Albin Hansson (Social Democrats)
1946 – 1951	Tage Erlander (Social Democrats)
1951 – 1957	Tage Erlander (Social Democrats and the Bondeförbundet)
1957 – 1969	Tage Erlander (Social Democrats)
1969 – 1976	Olof Palme
1976 – 1978	Thorbjörn Fälldin (Liberals and conservatives; Center party (formerly Bondeförbundet) Folkpartiet Liberalerna (the "Liberal People's party") and the Moderata Samlings-partiet (formerly "Högern")
1978 – 1979	Ola Ullsten (Folkpartiet Liberalerna)
1979 – 1981	Thorbjörn Fälldin (Liberals and conservatives; Center party (formerly Bondeförbundet) Folk party and the Moderata Samlingspartiet (formerly "Högern")
1981 – 1982	Thorbjörn Fälldin (Liberals; the Center party and Folkpariet)
1982 – 1986	Olof Palme (Social Democrats)
1986 – 1991	Ingvar Carlsson (Social Democrats)
1991 – 1994	Carl Bildt (Moderata Samlingspartiet, Center- and Folk-partiet and the Christian Democrats)
1994 – 1996	Ingvar Carlsson (Social Democrats)
1996 – 2006	Göran Persson (Social Democrats)
2006 -	Fredrik Reinfeldt (Moderata Samlingspartiet, Center- and Folkpartiet and the Christian Democrats)

Presidents in the United States of America

President	Years	Party
George Washington	1789-1797	
John Adams	1797-1801	Federalist
Thomas Jefferson	1801-1809	Democratic Republican
James Madison	1809-1817	Democratic Republican
James Monroe	1817-1825	Democratic Republican
John Quincy Adams	1825-1829	Democratic Republican
Andrew Jackson	1829-1837	D
Martin van Buren	1837-1841	D
William H Harrison	1841	Whig
John Tyler	1841-1845	Whig
James K Polk	1845-1849	D
Zachary Taylor	1849-1850	Whig
Millard Fillmore	1850-1853	Whig
Franklin Pierce	1853-1857	D
James Buchanan	1857-1861	D
Abraham Lincoln	1861-1865	R
Andrew Johnson	1865-1869	R
Ulysses S Grant	1869-1877	R
Rutherford Hayes	1877-1881	R
James Garfield	1881	R
Chester Arthur	1881-1885	R
Grover Cleveland	1885-1889	D
Benjamin Harrison	1889-1893	R
Grover Cleveland	1893-1897	D
William McKinley	1897-1901	R
Theodore Roosevelt	1901-1909	R
William Taft	1909-1913	R
Woodrow Wilson	1913-1921	D
Warren Harding	1921-1923	R
Calvin Coolidge	1923-1929	R
Herbert Hoover	1929-1933	R
Franklin D Roosevelt	1933-1945	D
Harry S Truman	1945-1953	D
Dwight D Eisenhower	1953-1961	R
John F Kennedy	1961-1963	D
Lyndon B Johnson	1963-1968	D
Richard Nixon	1969-1974	R
Gerald ford	1974-1977	R
Jimmy Carter	1977-1981	D
Ronald Reagan	1981-1989	R
George Bush	1989-1993	R
Bill Clinton	1993-2001	D
George W Bush	2001-2009	R